"With this book you can e:  al
and relatable way and gain :e
your team and others."
Mi ie
's

"A fascinating and practical ..... explores two big questions every manager and leader needs to answer. How do I get the best out of myself and how do I get the best from others? Curious to find out more? Then dive straight into this highly engaging read."
Professor Paul McGee – aka The Sumo Guy,
Sunday Times Best Selling Author and Motivational Speaker

"This book is a much-needed tool for leaders. Motivation is too often overlooked but remains the core fuel of performance in all our endeavours. Catherine lays out why motivation is so crucial to enabling a thriving workplace and explains how leaders can go about understanding and inspiring motivation in those they lead. Post-pandemic, these insights are more crucial than ever."
Cath Bishop, *Olympian, former Diplomat, Leadership Coach and Author of* The Long Win

"Grounded in rigorous psychological research, Catherine has created a fantastic resource for the 21st century leader. This practical guide helps readers to increase their own self-awareness and learn how to lead others to fulfil their potential."
Dr Penny Moyle, *Business Psychologist and Executive Coach, Highview Insights Ltd*

"The ambiguity around the future of the work place and the shift to virtual working have put pressures on leaders like never before. Both executives and employees at all levels are feeling lonely with side-effects such as depression and anxiety. In the midst of this context, it is vital for leaders to motivate their teams and the wider organisation. This book provides an excellent, simple to use tool kit for helping you to deliver results together with others."
Guy Lubitsh, *Professor in Leadership & Psychology, Hult Ashridge Executive Education*

"This really practical book explores how motivation influences self and others. By taking well known theories and bringing them to life through the experience of a range of managers, this book explores personal 'type' and how important it is to understand that the success of any task is dependent upon the people involved in delivering it. I'd recommend it for both newly appointed and experienced managers as an interesting and useful guide to understanding what motivates people."

Sue Higginson, *Principal and CEO, Wirral Met College*

"This book brings together content and real examples with the opportunity to pause and reflect about personal behaviour, choices, and aspirations. Each chapter encourages the reader's brain to slow down and learn thoughtfully, which is much needed in this current world of limited attention, fast responses and rapid problem-solving."

Dr Helena Boschi, *Psychologist and Applied Neuroscientist*

"Most leaders know that they are supposed to be 'different' from the old command and control, but they don't always know how. This book provides the guidance they need – it's an essential read for people managers at all levels."

Ashley Oates, *Market Area Director (Audi), Jardine Motors Group*

"Nearly every Team Leader finds that motivating and inspiring their people is a challenge and a learning journey. This easily accessible guide will help them with a range of tools and ideas from which they are sure to get invaluable help along that journey. Every new leader should receive this as a welcome present!"

Andrew Mayo, *Professor of Human Capital Management, Middlesex University*

"This book is a great resource for the leader in all of us. It reveals essential motivators that feed our psychological needs and provides practical ways to stretch beyond our own motivators to powerfully lead ourselves and others."

Linda Berens PhD, *Author of* Exploring Essential Motivators, *Founder, InterStrength™ Institute*

"This book provides readers with the opportunity to learn about motivation; this is accompanied by very informative self-assessments and tasks. The combination of knowledge, action and also reflection is highly commendable."

Dr Jennifer Johnson, *University of Liverpool Management School*

"This inspiring work provides a thorough exploration of communication and motivation as well as numerous practical tools and activities that can be used to facilitate personal and team development. Catherine Stothart has created a much needed practical guide that uses the lens of Temperament theory to help individuals understand their own core motivators and how to work effectively in a team. This book, based on extensive academic research and her decades of experience, is an essential resource for managers, coaches and facilitators seeking to motivate team members and build self-confidence."

Mary McGuiness, *Author of* You've Got Personality *and Director of the Institute for Type Development*

"This guidebook will show you exactly how to inspire and engage even the most challenging members of your team to find more fulfilment and enjoyment in their work and perform at their best! The relevant and relatable case examples really bring the material to life and the book captures the essence of the 'New Leader'."

Eve Delunas, *PhD, Author of* Survival Games Personalities Play

"Catherine's book is a simple, clear guide to understanding your leadership style by accepting that there are different temperaments in human personality, any one of which can mean success as a leader and where motivation will vary. The interactive 'exercises' are an engaging way of encouraging readers to work out the practical applications that will work for them."

Jenny Rogers, *Executive Coach and Writer*

"This is a thorough and well researched book and is an essential read for people managers at all levels. It's a great resource and provides valuable insights into how to shift perspectives for different situations. I highly recommend it."

Sue Blair, *Director of Personality Dynamics, Author, Speaker, Coach*

"This useful and timely coaching handbook is underpinned by Catherine's extensive experience of coaching leaders and managers. I recommend this book as a handy guide to anyone needing to motivate individuals and teams, whether leaders and managers or coaches and educators."

Lisa Rossetti, *Coach and Community Practitioner, co-author of* Story Skills for Managers: Nurturing Motivation with Teams, *Member of Association for Coaching*

"Motivation is a key factor in today's fast-changing work environment. Too often the talk about motivation is very general, missing what constitutes meaningful work for each individual. This book, based on Essential Motivators, (developed from Keirsey's work on Temperament), gives great insight into individuals' core needs, values, and talents and therefore what is likely to motivate them. It's a valuable resource for managers, coaches, consultants, and leaders to use both in relation to themselves and others."

Susan Nash, *Author, founder of The Type Academy and architect of Flawless Facilitation*

"Catherine is an expert on motivation. Her extensive research of relevant scenarios brings a beautiful real-life perspective to motivation. The concept of Leader-Manager is crucial to successful business leaders and can be transformative in the development of themselves and their teams. The case studies offer a phenomenal way to apply learning in a practical way. A must read for any leader of people!"

Brianna Burgos, *Senior Manager, People Development & Organizational Learning*

"Catherine has successfully integrated multiple complementary motivation frameworks which results in a comprehensive and powerful resource for leader-managers. Her insights on how to leverage the four motivation patterns are among the best I have seen. Every reader will discover motivational take-aways they can use themselves – and leave with clear techniques they can use with their teams."

Rob Toomey, *President, TypeCoach LLC*

"Catherine has a way of simplifying management models by using 'live' examples and then getting us to look more introspectively at both our own and others' styles. Bring out the best in yourself and others by buying this book!"

Jane Hubbard, *Director, People Jigsaw Ltd,*
former HR Director of Chester Zoo

MOTIVATION

Motivation is regarded as a cornerstone of performance in the workplace, both personally and for organisations. If you are a leader, manager, or HR professional, this book will show you how to tap into what motivates every individual so that you can enable them to use their talents and fulfil their potential. You will also learn more about your own motivation and how this impacts your leadership style.

Written by bestselling author and leadership coach, Catherine Stothart, this book captures the essence of motivation in an insightful and practical way. You will learn specific tools and techniques for four key management capabilities – how to engage, develop, delegate to, and connect with your teams. You will also find out how to sustain your own motivation and be resilient through setbacks.

Using activities, case studies, models, tools, tips, and templates for practical action, this book is ideal for those who want to know how to motivate their teams, improve their well-being, and feel motivated themselves. It is also invaluable to HR managers, executive and life coaches, and learning and development professionals.

Catherine Stothart has 30 years' experience in leadership development with top multinational companies – currently Airbus and Google. She has coached and trained hundreds of leaders in the private sector and in education to engage and motivate their teams and develop themselves.

MOTIVATION

THE ULTIMATE GUIDE TO LEADING YOUR TEAM

Catherine Stothart

LONDON AND NEW YORK

Cover design and illustration by Jason Emon of Emon Creative

First published 2023
by Routledge
4 Park Square, Milton Park, Abingdon, Oxon OX14 4RN

and by Routledge
605 Third Avenue, New York, NY 10158

Routledge is an imprint of the Taylor & Francis Group, an informa business

© 2023 Essenwood Consulting Ltd

The right of Catherine Stothart to be identified as author of this work has been asserted in accordance with sections 77 and 78 of the Copyright, Designs and Patents Act 1988.

All rights reserved. No part of this book may be reprinted or reproduced or utilised in any form or by any electronic, mechanical, or other means, now known or hereafter invented, including photocopying and recording, or in any information storage or retrieval system, without permission in writing from the publishers.

Trademark notice: Product or corporate names may be trademarks or registered trademarks, and are used only for identification and explanation without intent to infringe.

British Library Cataloguing-in-Publication Data
A catalogue record for this book is available from the British Library

Library of Congress Cataloging-in-Publication Data
Names: Stothart, Catherine, author.
Title: Motivation : the ultimate guide to leading your team / Catherine Stothart.
Description: Abingdon, Oxon ; New York, NY : Routledge, 2023. | Includes bibliographical references and index. | Identifiers: LCCN 2022021970 (print) | LCCN 2022021971 (ebook) | ISBN 9781032261287 (hbk) |
ISBN 9781032261300 (pbk) | ISBN 9781003286646 (ebk)
Subjects: LCSH: Employee motivation. | Leadership. | Management. | Teams in the workplace.
Classification: LCC HF5549.5.M63 S765 2023 (print) | LCC HF5549.5.M63 (ebook) | DDC 658.3/14—dc23/eng/20220525
LC record available at https://lccn.loc.gov/2022021970
LC ebook record available at https://lccn.loc.gov/2022021971

ISBN: 978-1-032-26128-7 (hbk)
ISBN: 978-1-032-26130-0 (pbk)
ISBN: 978-1-003-28664-6 (ebk)

DOI: 10.4324/9781003286646

Typeset in Bembo
by codeMantra

To the leader in all of us.

CONTENTS

About the Author		xvii
Preface		xix
Acknowledgements		xxi
Introduction		1
Who This Book Is For 1		
Why You Need Motivation 1		
Management and Motivation 3		
Management and Well-being 4		
Navigating the Motivation Minefield 5		
How You Can Use This Book 6		
1	What Are Motivation and Purpose?	9
	Introduction 9	
	What Is Motivation? 10	
	Motivation and Well-being 14	
	Purpose 15	
	Four Needs – The Core Motivators 19	
	Persistence and Resilience 22	
	The Leader-Manager's Role 24	
	Summary 28	
	Action Plan 29	
2	What's Your Purpose? – How to Find Your "Why"	31
	Introduction 31	
	Self-Insight Activity 1 32	
	Self-Insight Activity 2 34	

Self-Insight Activity 3 35
Summary So Far 36
Quiz 37
Decision Time! 43
Summary 45
Action Plan 46

3 One Size Doesn't Fit All – The Four Core Motivators 47
Introduction 47
The Improviser Motivation Pattern 48
The Stabiliser Motivation Pattern 54
The Theorist Motivation Pattern 61
The Catalyst Motivation Pattern 67
Summary 74
Action Plan 74

4 Leading on Purpose 76
Introduction 76
Engage to Give Meaning 77
Develop to Build Competence 85
Delegate to Give Freedom 90
Connect to Create Belonging 92
Tips for the Top Motivators 97
Summary 100
Action Plan 100

5 Persistence and Performance 102
Introduction 102
What Is Persistence? 103
The Leader-Manager's Role 109
Setting Motivating Goals 109
Giving Feedback That Works 113
Coaching to Build Self-Belief 116
Doing It Virtually 120
Creating a Culture of Persistence 121
Tips for the Top Motivators 121
Summary 124
Action Plan 124

6 **Helpful Habits and Resilient Behaviours**   126
Introduction 126
What Is Resilience? 127
Energy 127
What Is Stress? 132
The Leader-Manager's Role 134
Tips for the Top Motivators 140
Summary 143
Action Plan 143

7 **Up Close and Personal – Leading and Working with Others**   145
Introduction 145
Leadership Styles 145
Engaging and Connecting with Your Team 151
Tips for the Top Motivators – Connecting 159
Dealing with Conflict 161
Tips for the Top Motivators – Defusing Conflict 166
Developing Yourself 167
Summary 170
Action Plan 170

Appendix   172
Appendix Contents 172
Lookup Table of the Four Motivation Patterns 172
Motivation Theories 176
Overview of Temperament Theory 179
Self-assessment Questionnaires 181

Index   183

ABOUT THE AUTHOR

Photo by Szabolcs Pajor of ZNN Photo Artistry

Catherine Stothart is a Leadership Coach with 30 years' experience in leadership development with top multinational companies – currently Airbus and Google, and previously including Audi, Astra Zeneca, and United Utilities. She has coached and trained hundreds of leaders in the private sector and in education to engage and motivate their teams and develop themselves.

She delivers workshops (in-person and online) to management teams and speaks to professional groups. Catherine previously held posts in HR and Learning and Development in Ford Motor Company, Mercury Communications, and ICL.

Catherine has lived in Egypt and Brazil and now lives in Chester, UK. Living overseas really opened her eyes to human behaviour and cultural differences. Her work has continued with this underlying theme of behavioural change and personal development ever since.

She is widely connected with an international network – in Europe, the USA, Australia, and New Zealand – through her role as Director of Events for the British Association of Psychological Type (BAPT), a charitable organisation whose aim is to bring knowledge of personality type to a wider audience to enrich lives. She speaks at conferences internationally, both in person and online.

Catherine is a Chartered Fellow of the Chartered Institute of Personnel and Development, has an MSc in Organisational Behaviour from Birkbeck College, University of London, has a BA in English from the University of Oxford, and has qualifications in Coaching, MBTI® Steps 1 and 2, and other psychometric instruments.

She is the author of *How to Get On with Anyone: Gain the Confidence and Charisma to Communicate with Any Personality Type* (2018, Pearson) – a guide to building better relationships with others, at work or at home. She has also written an e-book, *Communicating with Positive Impact and Influence* (2021, Bookboon).

In her spare time, Catherine plays tennis, cycles, attends live sport, music, and theatre, and spends as much time out of doors as possible.

PREFACE

WHY I WROTE THIS BOOK

Part way through my career in human resource management, I took a pause to study for a Master's degree. I had worked for nearly 20 years in blue-chip companies and had experienced many ideas, policies, and practices for managing and motivating people. There were new buzzwords, like engagement. I wanted to find out how much of what we did in organisations was based on sound theory and evidence. What I found was that there is a lot of valuable knowledge in the academic world which is not always easily translated into practice in organisations.

Since then, I have made it my mission to bring some of the best thinking about communication and motivation to a wider audience in a way that makes it usable and actionable. I do this through my work as a Leadership Coach, through team workshops and speaking engagements, and through my books.

My first book, *How to Get On with Anyone* (2018, Pearson), was about how to be emotionally intelligent when you interact with other people – how to be more self-aware and aware of others so that you can adapt your behaviour to connect with them and get better results for all.

In *Motivation: The Ultimate Guide to Leading Your Team*, I go deeper – into our core motivators, why we do what we do, why we choose certain things and not others, and what really makes us feel fulfilled and gives us a sense of self-worth.

I draw on academic research, interviews with colleagues in business and education, experts and writers, and my experience as a leadership coach and trainer. I want to bring the best thinking about motivation to a wide audience because I believe that if you know what motivates you and others, you can be more effective and fulfilled at work and meet the challenge of engaging and inspiring others.

ACKNOWLEDGEMENTS

Many people have contributed to the creation of this book and my gratitude goes to all of them. Here are some specific thanks and appreciation to:

Susan Nash for inviting me to join her Type Academy seven years ago – Susan and the international members of the Type Academy have been a wonderful source of learning and knowledge sharing and I could not have written this book without their inspiration.

The people who so generously gave their time to be interviewed about their experiences of motivation – in particular, Phil Bradshaw, Helen Bradley, Jennifer Johnson, Ashley Oates, Tim Casserley, Sue Higginson, Amy Capstick, and Brianna Burgos.

The people who equally generously took the time to read the first draft and give me very helpful feedback and suggestions, most of which I adopted in the final version – Andrew Mayo, Sue Blair, Helen Bradley, Eve Delunas, Teresa Moon, Richard Moulds, and Judy Moulds.

Jason Emon of Emon Creative for his patience and skill in exploring my thoughts and then coming up with creative illustrations to express them.

Alison Jones of Practical Inspiration Publishing whose Extraordinary Business Book Club Campfire and the authors who attend it were (and are) a valued source of support, encouragement, and practical tips.

Alison Smith, a good friend and excellent proof reader who willingly gave her time and attention to detail to checking drafts, correcting errors, and suggesting improvements.

My editor, Rebecca Marsh, and Assistant Editor, Lauren Whelan, for their advice and guidance throughout the complex process of writing, producing, and marketing a book.

Linda Berens, for sharing her extensive knowledge and for allowing me to use her labels for the four core motivators. Improviser™, Stabilizer™, Theorist™, and Catalyst™, as described in *Exploring Essential Motivators*™ by Linda V. Berens, InterStrength Press, Huntington Beach, California, are used with the permission of Linda V. Berens.

All the leaders and managers from whom I have learned so much over many years about the practicalities and challenges of leading others.

Finally, my gratitude goes to my husband, Bill Stothart, for his unfailing love and support throughout our lives together and for his motivation in building a wildlife pond while I was writing this book during COVID lockdowns!

INTRODUCTION

WHO THIS BOOK IS FOR

This book is for leaders and managers of people who want to know how to motivate their teams, improve their well-being, and feel motivated themselves.

You will:

- Learn how to tap into your team's core motivators and lead them to fulfil their purpose and potential
- Find out how to manage others in a way that enhances their well-being
- Understand more about your own motivation so you can make choices about your career and life that fit with who you really are

It is also a valuable resource for HR Managers, Executive and Life Coaches, and Learning and Development professionals.

WHY YOU NEED MOTIVATION

> In order that people may be happy in their work, these three things are needed: they must be fit for it; they must not do too much of it; and they must have a sense of success in it.
> *John Ruskin*[1]

Although Ruskin wrote those words over 150 years ago, they are still relevant today. Using our skills, having work-life balance, and feeling good about our work are important for motivation and well-being.

DOI: 10.4324/9781003286646-1

There are other things too that we need if we are to feel motivated:

- To have some choice and control in how we do our jobs
- To belong to the group and feel valued for contributing to it
- To use our talents and know we are good at our jobs
- To fulfil our potential and help others fulfil theirs

No one tells you how to motivate yourself or how to motivate others – you are expected to work it out for yourself. Many people never find out what really motivates them. They get bound up in being busy, in meeting demands and pressures from others, while leaving little time for doing the things that make them feel positive, confident, and truly themselves.

Yet being motivated is at the core of who we are. Motivation at work affects all of us, but few people really understand it and do not fulfil their potential.

One of my interviewees for this book[2] describes a "pivot point" in his career when he was offered an opportunity by his manager to study for a postgraduate diploma in Business Administration. Through this he learned more about leadership, "discovered a passion for developing people," and made a career change from leading a technical team to developing leaders. A brave choice, but one that paid off.

If you know what motivates you, you can make choices about your life and career that enable you to do more of those things and draw on that motivation to fulfil your sense of purpose, leading to greater happiness and well-being.[3]

If you manage others, you can do so in a way that enables them to give their best – engaging and inspiring them by tapping into their core motivation and leading them to fulfil their potential. They will be more productive and get more enjoyment from their work. What could be better than that? This is why motivation – for both your team and you – is so important.

It is often said that when people leave an organisation, they are resigning from their manager, rather than from the company. An alternative view, from research at Facebook,[4] is that people leave when "their job wasn't enjoyable, their strengths weren't being used, and they weren't growing in their careers." These are all things that managers can control and influence.

MANAGEMENT AND MOTIVATION

Tapping into your own and your team's motivation is a key capability for managers. But not everyone is motivated at work:

- Twenty-nine percent of employees say they are not motivated at work[5]
- Gallup reports that 80% of employees are not engaged at work[6]
- Just 15% of employees feel their employer is trying to understand what motivates them[7]

The Chartered Institute of Personnel and Development (CIPD) reports that motivated employees are essential for business success:

> Employees who have good quality jobs and are managed well, will not only be happier, healthier and more fulfilled, but are also more likely to drive productivity, better products or services, and innovation.[8]

The days of "command and control" management are long gone. Our organisations are more complex and our society more sophisticated. People expect more from work than just doing what the boss says. And indeed, in bringing their whole selves to work, they contribute more and feel more fulfilled. The role of the manager is not only to solve problems and make decisions so that the work gets done but also **to manage the human behaviours and relationships, the thoughts and feelings that exist in the workplace**.

What people expect of their manager is evolving, partly due to the COVID-19 pandemic. This made people question their assumptions about work. Large numbers of people worked from home, sometimes trying to home-school their children too. Flexible working and home working, which had been growing gradually, became the norm for many office workers. We started to rethink our values and re-evaluate how work fits into our lives.

It is estimated that 46% of the workforce will work partly from home,[9] making it more difficult for managers to engage and inspire people individually or create team spirit. In this environment, the manager becomes less of an overseer of task completion and more of an **enabler of self-motivation**.

Alongside the move to hybrid working, there are also generational changes. Increasingly, Gen Z (born since 1997) report a desire for careers with a positive impact on society and the environment. They want to work for organisations that prioritise social responsibility. They also look for flexibility in how and when they work – as well as where – and they want fulfilment from their work.[10]

MANAGEMENT AND WELL-BEING

Employees, and especially millennials (born 1981–1996), want their managers to be more supportive and "empathic," someone who is concerned about their well-being.[11] People are now much more open about problems with mental health. It is estimated that at any given time, one in six working-age adults in the UK have symptoms associated with mental ill health.[12] Young people – the future workforce – appear to be experiencing more difficulties than previously and are more willing to talk about it. But:

- Only 35% of employees believe that work has a positive impact on their mental health (CIPD Good Work Index 2022)
- Only 26% said their employer was genuinely concerned about their well-being (Living to Work survey 2018)

A Gallup survey[13] of Gen Z and millennials found that the two most important things they want from organisations are that they care about well-being and demonstrate ethical leadership. Many current managers are millennials, so we can expect that they will want to manage others and be managed themselves differently from their predecessors. This book is a guide to doing that.

Motivation and well-being are closely related – tapping into what motivates each person enables them to use their talents and fulfil their potential, and this can improve their overall well-being and happiness. The key question for managers is no longer

- *how can I get the most out of people?*

But rather:

- *how can I support people to perform at their best and fulfil their potential?*

One of my interviewees[14] for this book describes the changes in the retail motor industry:

> In the past Sales Executives could be accused of being preoccupied with money, status and having the best car, but there has been a shift; they now are less motivated by financial reward and are more concerned with work-life balance, a 5-day week, a nice car but not necessarily the best – they are more tuned into their own mental state and have a greater awareness of well-being. They want a conversation with a boss who is more genuine, caring, empathetic, and sympathetic, expecting their voice to be heard, so that they are both listened to and respected.

NAVIGATING THE MOTIVATION MINEFIELD

It's tough for managers. We place the responsibility for motivating and engaging people on managers, but they often have little training for this. The Chartered Management Institute in the UK estimates that up to four out of five (2.4 million) bosses in Britain are "accidental managers" – people who have technical training but are untrained in management.[15]

It is challenging for managers to navigate this minefield of responsibilities and expectations and fulfil their own potential too. But it is not impossible – allocating time to improving people skills is essential to good leadership. The consequences of poor management can be detrimental to the managers themselves, their teams, and their organisations.

Motivation has been studied for many years, and it continues to puzzle and fascinate people. It is the Holy Grail for psychologists – if only we knew what motivates people, they would work harder, get more done, be happier, have greater resilience, be less susceptible to poor mental health, and so on. In fact, much **is** known in the academic world about what gives people purpose and motivation. But this valuable knowledge has not filtered through to the broader population in a way that makes it usable and actionable.

Motivation: The Ultimate Guide to Leading Your Team bridges the gap between academic theory and management practice.

- You will find guidance on your role as a people manager in relation to your team and especially your role in creating the conditions for people to be motivated and have well-being
- You will discover the core motivators – freedom, competence, belonging, and fulfilling potential – and what that means for how you lead people and for what your team needs from you
- You will learn how to tap into the core motivators with specific guidance in four key management capability areas – how to engage, develop, delegate to, and connect with your team more effectively
- You will find simple tools and techniques to help your team (and you) sustain your motivation and be resilient through setbacks
- You will realise how your own top motivator impacts your leadership style and how to flex it to enable colleagues to harness their own motivation and maintain their well-being

HOW YOU CAN USE THIS BOOK

Motivation is a combination of purpose, persistence, and resilience, and the book covers these in sequence, linking theory to practical approaches.

Chapter 1: summarises relevant theories and frameworks to give insight and confidence in the practices that are recommended in later chapters.

Chapters 2 and 3: enable the reader to explore their own motivation and sense of purpose through self-insight activities, a quiz, descriptions, and case studies.

Chapter 4: covers the first component of motivation – purpose – and the practical tools to engage, develop, delegate to, and connect with people to tap into their sense of purpose.

Chapters 5 and 6: cover the other components of motivation – persistence and resilience – and the management practices, such as setting goals, giving feedback and coaching, that enable these in others.

Chapter 7: discusses how your motivation impacts how you lead others and what they might need from you.

Read the book from cover to cover to get the most out of it. Alternatively, you can use it as a handbook and dip into the parts that you need most now. If you want to find out more about your own leadership style, read Chapters 1–3 and then 7. If you want practical guidance on specific situations, concentrate on Chapters 4–6.

The chapters include real-life case studies, mostly with names changed. Some case studies come from the people I interviewed for this book.

Self-assessment tools, models, and templates are used throughout the book. They are available in a Workbook as a free download from my website www.essenwood.co.uk.

The Appendix includes a lookup table with the key characteristics of each motivation pattern. There is also a summary of the most important theories of motivation and temperament theory, with references for anyone who wants to know more.

NOTES

1. Ruskin, J. (1851) *Pre-Raphaelitism*. Chichester: Wiley.
2. Phil Bradshaw, Talent and Executive Management Coordinator UK, Airbus.
3. https://theconversation.com/having-a-sense-of-meaning-in-life-is-good-for-you-so-how-do-you-get-one-110361.
4. Goler, L., Gale, J., Harrington, B., and Grant, A. (2018). "Why People Really Quit Their Jobs," *Harvard Business Review*, January 2018.
5. Living to Work Survey 2018.
6. The Gallup State of the Global Workplace 2021 Report.
7. Aviva/Robertson Cooper survey "Embracing the Age of Ambiguity" (2020).
8. CIPD factsheet *Employee Engagement and Motivation*, 2019.
9. Gartner (2021), https://www.gartner.com/en/human-resources/trends/remote-work-revolution.
10. CFA Institute Graduate Outlook Survey 2021 reported in *People Management* December 2021.
11. *Harvard Business Review* Survey 2021.
12. https://mhfaengland.org/mhfa-centre/research-and-evaluation/mental-health-statistics/. McManus, S., Bebbington, P., Jenkins, R.,

Brugha, T. (2016). Mental health and wellbeing in England: Adult Psychiatric Morbidity Survey 2014 [Internet]. Leeds. Available from: content.digital.nhs.uk.
13 https://www.gallup.com/workplace/336275/things-gen-millennials-expect-workplace.aspx.
14 Ashley Oates, Market Area Director (Audi), Jardine Motors Group.
15 Chartered Management Institute (2017). *Leadership for Change: CMI's Management Manifesto*. London: Chartered Management Institute.

WHAT ARE MOTIVATION AND PURPOSE?

INTRODUCTION

Most days I get up in the morning and am really looking forward to the day and the things I am going to do. But some days I'm not so keen – and usually this is because there is something I know I should do but really don't feel like doing, and this casts a shadow over the day. Wouldn't it be great if I could have more of the good days and fewer of the others?

We lead busy lives with many demands on us, and there is little time to stop to think about what really motivates us and makes us feel good about ourselves. Many people are not aware of what motivates them and may choose jobs that do not draw on their motivation or use their talents. Charles Darwin is a classic example of this – he initially studied to be a doctor but, fortunately for science, he neglected his medical education to study invertebrates.

This chapter answers questions such as:

- What is motivation, and is it the same as purpose?
- Why is having purpose important?
- How does being motivated relate to our mental and physical health and well-being?
- What are the four core motivators that drive our behaviour?
- How are motivation and engagement connected?
- And what is the manager's role in motivating the team and the individuals in it?

DOI: 10.4324/9781003286646-2

WHAT IS MOTIVATION?

Motivation is why we do what we do – what drives our actions. Having a sense of purpose, a reason for doing something, is part of motivation. This can be our internal drives, and it can also be the external stimulants to action, such as the demands of our jobs, our bosses, our home lives, things we feel we "should" do, things that other people require us to do, our roles in life, and, of course, the rewards and recognition we get for our actions. All these can act as motivators, but it is usually the internal drives (known as intrinsic motivation) that are **most** motivating, because they are connected to our sense of self. When we can fulfil those internal drives, we are likely to feel a sense of well-being and happiness.

Sometimes we can feel tension between our internal drives that propel us towards wanting to do something and the demands and rewards coming from outside that pressure us in other directions. We usually think of rewards as a good thing and in many cases they are. However, sometimes rewards, such as a big salary, can push us in directions that don't really fit with our core needs and who we really are (Figure 1.1).

Similarly, we often do things because we feel we "should" do them, that it is what is expected of us, but this can undermine our motivation and well-being.

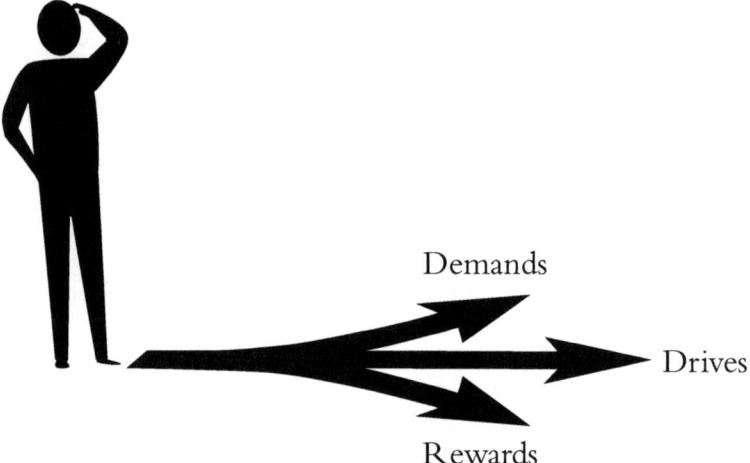

Figure 1.1 Demands, Rewards, and Drives

This is a surprisingly common problem, which people often encounter in midlife, and it is expressed here in a letter written to a problem page in a newspaper:

> I am realising that I have spent so much time trying to do what is expected of me that I have absolutely no idea what it is that I want to do.

In this case, the letter writer was advised to "internally reference more, that means working out how things feel to you, and do less external referencing – which is how things look to others."[1] In other words, cast aside the "shoulds," and think about how you really feel about your work and what aspects of it give you meaning or enjoyment.

At the heart of motivation is intrinsic motivation,[2] not the external things that might make you feel good for a short time – a high salary or the things that money can buy – a car, a house, new clothes, holidays. These can give you a sense of motivation for a short time, but it soon wears off. What really motivates in the long term is the things that you *do* – how you spend your time at work and at home – that make you feel fulfilled. Things that relate to your inner sense of personal purpose. Things that meet your psychological needs. Things that feel part of your identity, who you are as a person.

Here are some examples of extrinsic and intrinsic motivators. The external stimulants are often things that are done to you, while the inner drives are more often what you choose to do.

External Stimulants	*Inner Drives / Core Needs*
Demands from others	Things you enjoy doing
Expectations of what you "should" do	Things that lead to fulfilment
Rewards:	Needs for:
Salary and benefits	Being competent
Praise and recognition	Having some freedom and choice
Promotion	Belonging to a group
Status	Fulfilling potential

All of these, and more, can motivate us and move us to action. But the intrinsic motivators are the most motivating and long-lasting. Among these are four core needs – for competence, freedom, belonging, and fulfilling potential – that people share, and which drive their action, to varying degrees and with different relative importance. There are also other individual factors that influence intrinsic motivation too, such as our values, our interests, our upbringing, and culture. Each of us is an individual, but there are common patterns we share with others. Knowing about these common patterns makes it easier to motivate ourselves or others while recognising that it does not explain everything about motivation.

If we can meet these four needs, then we have much more chance of feeling motivated and reaching our potential. If you manage others, then you can help them find ways to meet those needs through their work.

Fulfilling these four needs is part of our sense of purpose. They apply to a greater or lesser extent to all of us and are discussed later in this chapter.

> *David* had always been good at science at school. His teachers and parents encouraged him to use his aptitude for Science by applying to study Medicine at university. He enjoyed most of the course, especially the theoretical aspects, and he completed his qualifications and joined a GP practice. He was good at diagnosing the health problems brought to him by his patients and liked to keep up to date on new therapies and approaches. But he often felt stressed at the end of the day. He realised that while he enjoyed applying his medical knowledge, he did not enjoy the interactions with patients – an important aspect of being a GP. He moved to a medical role in a pharmaceutical company where he could focus on the technical aspects of his role and was able to use his talents for analysing and innovating more fully.

Motivation is about what drives your choice of what to do, and it is also about how hard you try and how long you keep trying.[3] It is **a combination of PURPOSE, PERSISTENCE, and RESILIENCE.**

Sometimes there are obstacles and barriers to overcome. Some of these barriers are our own self-limiting beliefs or inability to organise our lives. This book is also about the practicalities of setting goals,

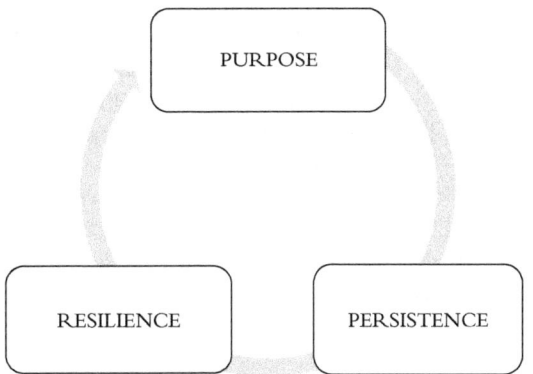

Figure 1.2 Motivation: Purpose, Persistence, and Resilience

prioritising, developing helpful beliefs, and looking after our physical and mental health – all the things that help you maintain your **persistence** and **resilience** (Figure 1.2).

Summary of Terms

Motivation: why we do what we do – what causes us to act, both external and internal stimulants, including our inner needs and drives.

Being motivated and sustaining motivation require at least these three things:

Purpose:

- Having something meaningful to you which moves you to action
- An inner drive to fulfil your needs for competence, freedom, belonging, and fulfilling potential

Persistence: managing your thoughts, beliefs, and emotions to keep making efforts towards a course of action, despite difficulties or opposition from others.

Resilience: taking care of your energy needs to recover from challenges and setbacks and maintain a positive outlook.

MOTIVATION AND WELL-BEING

When we have a meaningful purpose that relates to our core needs, we can get into a "flow"[4] state and be both productive and happy. Many of the things that help us persist and be resilient are the same things that enable our well-being. Motivation and well-being are two sides of the same coin – each contributes to the other.

When we are in touch with what motivates us and can spend time on those things, we feel happier and more confident and have a greater sense of well-being. Spending too much time and effort on things that drain our energy demotivates us, undermines our sense of self-worth, and decreases our well-being.

> **Amy**[5] did a Law degree and was expected to go into the legal profession or join a consultancy. She says she "blindly followed this path" and joined a consultancy as a tax advisor. "To begin with I am learning new things and meeting new people and that keeps me relatively entertained." But after three years, she got frustrated and started "acting out" with managers. She says she also became difficult with her partner and friends outside work. Assuming the problem was with her colleagues, she joined a different consultancy in the same field.
> She liked the team but after nine months,
>
>> I am crawling the walls, watching the clock, not wanting to go to work and I realise it's not who I work for, it's what I'm doing. ... And then it clicks for me, I'm bored. I am so bored and I do not care about tax. I don't care at all. And I think about the rest of my working life, 40 something years of doing the same thing over and over every year and I'm like ... nope, can't do it, not going to. ... I want a career with way more day to day variety, I know I'm much better in the moment than over long projects or pieces of work and the most unpredictable thing I know of at that point is HR. I also wanted to be contributing to the business I work for.
>
> Amy changed career and sees her regular promotions since then as evidence that she performs much better in a role that fits her motivation pattern.

Ahmed found his work role didn't fit his inner core motivation.

> **Ahmed** joined a bank after he left university. He knew it would offer a good career with excellent benefits and a pleasant working environment. He enjoyed the training scheme and found his job as a Customer Account Manager interesting. But he had a nagging sense that something was missing – it was a well-paid job, he liked his colleagues, but he didn't feel inspired. He eventually realised that what he really wanted to do in his job was to help people personally in a practical way, and while the bank's customers appreciated his advice, he couldn't help them as individuals. After much soul-searching, he decided to retrain as a physiotherapist. This turned out to be a great decision – he absolutely loved his work, he was able to help people in a practical and personal way, and he felt valued by his patients.

Amy and Ahmed found jobs that tapped into what was important to them, and they felt motivated and happier.

Take a pause here to reflect on what moves you to action – why do you do what you do?

Notes

The next sections look in more detail at purpose, persistence, and resilience.

PURPOSE

Why We Need Purpose

> Most of us live our lives by accident. Fulfilment comes when we live our lives on purpose.[6] *Simon Sinek*

Having a sense of purpose is fundamental to existence. Indeed, if you are in dire circumstances – a refugee for example – then your personal purpose **is** to survive, and this becomes your primary focus. If you can satisfy your needs at the basic level of existence, then you will look to fulfil other, higher-level needs such as relationships with others and personal growth, as noted by Alderfer[7] – these give our lives meaning and lead to greater mental and emotional well-being.

Human beings need meaning and purpose in their lives. A study of people who retire suggests that "26% of retirees later unretire."[8] Explaining this, the author, Harvard University economist, Nicole Maestas, says "you have certain themes: a sense of purpose, using your brain, and another key component is social engagement."

For many people, work provides a sense of purpose, and the London Business School Leadership Institute Survey of 2017 concluded that:

> Put simply, people have to feel good about their work and understand how they, as an individual, are making a unique contribution to something bigger and meaningful.

Feeling that our work is meaningful is especially important, because we spend a lot of time at work, and, to some extent, our work persona becomes part of our sense of identity.

We need a sense of purpose outside work too. Neuroscientist Daniel Levitin says:

> Too much time spent with no purpose is associated with unhappiness. Stay busy! But not with busy work or trivial pursuits, but with meaningful activities.[9]

It must be the right type of activity – just being busy is not sufficient to give our lives a sense of purpose and happiness – it must connect with what motivates us and is meaningful for us.

Johan had retired from his role as a Finance Director at a manufacturing company. He had always felt responsible for the success of the company, he had a strong sense of loyalty to his colleagues, and he felt he belonged and was recognised for his contribution. When he first retired, he enjoyed having time to play golf and travel, but after a while, he began to feel that his life lacked the sense of purpose he got from belonging to and contributing to an organisation with others. He heard about a community charity that needed a driver to take elderly people to a social lunch club each week. He contacted them and became a volunteer driver. He felt much happier being part of a team doing something worthwhile. He had found a way to meet his core needs to do his duty and belong to a group.

Psychologists Danckert and Eastwood[10] noted the different reactions of two astronauts in space – one was totally bored and couldn't wait to get back to Earth, while the other felt satisfied carrying out routine maintenance tasks. Although the tasks were not interesting, they fulfilled his need to be dutiful and responsible and play his part in the team – this kept him motivated. The authors suggest a healthy response to boredom is to find something that engages our curiosity and capacities.

> Boredom is not an absence of things to do, it's the struggle to find value in any of the options available to you. Being able to connect with a reason "why" for doing something can make it less boring.[11]

People sometimes say they are motivated by "achievement" and that their desire to achieve something motivates them to work towards it. The experience of people in sport suggests that there is usually some other motivation behind this. Catherine Bishop[12] (former British rower who, with Katherine Grainger, was World Champion in the coxless pair in 2003 and, in 2004, won a silver medal at the Olympic Games) talks about needing a sense of core purpose and "finding the why" that goes beyond the short-term goal of winning a race. She describes the sense of emptiness that some athletes feel after winning because it doesn't connect to a deeper meaning and sense of purpose over the longer term.

The desire to achieve something (e.g. pass an exam, win a race, have the highest sales, design a new product) motivates you to work towards it – but **why** do you want to achieve it?

- Is it because it will lead to something else that you value?
- Is it because of what it shows about you if you achieve it?
- Is it because it will make a difference to other people?
- Is it because you want to do well for your team?
- Is it simply because you enjoy the activity itself?
- What does the achievement really mean to you?
- What makes the goal personally valuable to you?

> ***Jenny's***[13] story of how she was motivated to achieve her "very challenging goal" of a doctorate illustrates the profound impact of having a motivating purpose together with ways to persist and be resilient. She says her core motivator is "reaching my potential and that of others." During her research, she felt a "keen responsibility" and a "personal obligation" to enabling the voices of her participants to be heard – this was her "clear purpose" that motivated her. Being able to help others achieve their aspirations was important to her and gave her a sense of purpose. What helped her to persist was having "an end goal" and "accountability meetings with her supervisors." Finally, she says that "another aspect of my resilience was the supportive structure surrounding me … my two academic supervisors but also my immediate family."

The COVID-19 pandemic in 2020 deprived many people of the opportunity to do things that normally motivated them. One example was the cancellation of the end of school exams for 16- and 18-year-old pupils in the UK. Many were devastated and felt that everything they had been working towards had been taken away and there was nothing to give their lives a sense of purpose. Similarly, people who were laid off work with pay found it hard to motivate themselves. Even people who weren't employed before the pandemic found life under lockdown difficult, as the things that they used to do that gave their lives meaning were no longer available.

Lewis Pugh,[14] an ocean advocate and the first person to swim in every ocean in the world, in extremely physically and mentally challenging conditions, talks about "the power of having a purpose," which keeps him going. His purpose, which drives and sustains him while training for and doing the swims, is to raise awareness of the climate emergency and to get environmental protection for the oceans.

> Connect with your purpose, and this enables you to be successful.

Your sense of purpose may be short or long term, it may change over time, it may relate to your work or your life outside work, but **it will also be influenced by the enduring psychological**

needs of your personality, including the four core needs noted previously: having some freedom and choice, feeling competent, belonging to a group, and fulfilling potential. The inner drive to fulfil these needs underlies and motivates your actions – it gives you purpose. You will explore these needs through the activities in the next chapter. These four needs apply to a greater or lesser extent to all of us.

FOUR NEEDS – THE CORE MOTIVATORS

Most motivation theories broadly fall into two categories: the *content* of WHAT motivates us, which gives us a sense of purpose and reason for doing something, and the *processes* of HOW we are motivated.

The best-known *content* theory is Abraham Maslow's hierarchy of needs[15] and his idea that the most important motivator, once more basic needs are satisfied, is "self-actualisation." Researchers now believe that there are at least three types of needs that motivate all of us. According to Ryan and Deci's self-determination theory,[16] these are:

- Competence (being good at what we do)
- Autonomy (having some choice and freedom)
- Relatedness (having connections with other people)

I refer to these needs as the need for **competence**, the need for **freedom**, and the need for **belonging**. There is an additional need, recognised in temperament theory[17] – the need to have **meaning and fulfil potential** (Maslow's "self-actualisation"). While we share all four of these needs, we each have one that is more important to us.

Ryan and Deci make an explicit link between motivation and well-being:

> Three innate psychological needs – competence, autonomy, and relatedness – which when satisfied yield enhanced self-motivation and mental health and when thwarted lead to diminished motivation and well-being.[18]

If we can meet these needs in our work and our lives, we are more likely to feel motivated and have a sense of well-being. **As a** manager, you can give people opportunities to fulfil these needs through their work.

While these four needs matter to everyone, for each of us as individuals, their *relative* importance differs. Our personal route to fulfilment could be primarily through freedom, **or** through competence, **or** through belonging, **or**, as Maslow said, through self-actualisation (which I refer to as potential). These different core needs lead to different patterns of behaviour. (I am indebted for this idea to Linda Berens[19]). There will be individual factors too to add to the mix.

Ryan and Deci's theory of self-determination has parallels with another set of ideas about motivation and behaviour – the four temperaments.[20] This has a long history, and different writers have used different names for the four temperaments. Here I use the Berens' names. We can use the knowledge and insights from temperament theory, to enhance our understanding of **what the needs – the core motivators – mean in practice for behaviour, performance, and leadership style.**

This is how the two theories link together:

People motivated by:

Core Needs / Core Motivators		*Name*
Competence	Want to reach mastery and contribute to progress	Theorist™
Freedom	Want the freedom to act and get impressive quick results	Improviser™
Belonging	Want to do their duty for the group and be responsible	Stabiliser™
Potential	Want to be true to themselves and help others be the best they can be	Catalyst™

In your role as a manager, your own top motivator influences how you see your priorities and where your best contribution can come from.

Here is an example of how these different motivators can play out for leaders. In this case, each of the four people worked as a Head of Business of a luxury car dealership. All four heads of business were successful in their roles but displayed different strengths related to their different top motivators.

> *Abdul* was motivated by the need to have *freedom* to act and be able to get impressive quick results. He had his "finger on the pulse," knew exactly what was going on around him, and acted quickly to deal with problems. He was quick witted and able to think on his feet. He easily built rapport with customers, and he enjoyed being around the luxury cars in the showroom.
>
> *Gemma* was motivated by the need for *competence*, and her priority was to run an efficient and effective operation that would be seen as a benchmark for others. She promoted her site as the proving ground for using new technology, both in its customer-facing side and in the back-office activities.
>
> *Mike* was motivated by taking responsibility and *belonging* to a group. He had a reputation for being reliable, delivering what he said he would, following through on actions, and picking up tasks that no one else wanted to do. He liked to feel that he was keeping the wheels of the organisation turning.
>
> *Shanta* was motivated by her desire to help others fulfil their *potential*. She always had time for her team members and made it a priority to give feedback and coach them. She felt fulfilled when they went on to bigger roles. She was quick to pick up on any signs that people were not happy and dealt with this sensitively.

All four Heads of Business were successful in their roles, but their different inner motivators were linked to different talents, and this meant they each brought a different focus and approach to their roles and to their teams.

Our core motivator does not constrain us to always behave in certain ways – as people grow and develop, they broaden out from their core, becoming more aware of the strengths of other approaches and building in other skills to become more rounded human beings. This means that as managers, our notions of other people need to adapt to their growth too.

Being motivated differently from your own boss or from your team members can lead to communication difficulties and to a lack of appreciation of each other's talents.

PERSISTENCE AND RESILIENCE

As well as sense of purpose, **motivation is also about being persistent and resilient**. Lewis Pugh[21] talks about other key components of motivation: "grit, determination, resilience." Similarly, Max Whitlock,[22] the most successful British male artistic gymnast, 2016 double Olympic champion and winner of three world titles, talks about "determination and resilience," which kept him motivated to work hard despite setbacks.

The four core motivators are about the *content* of WHAT motivates us, why we do what we do, the needs we want to fulfil, which give purpose to our actions. Sustaining motivation – being persistent and resilient – is about the *processes* of motivation – HOW we are motivated, the tools and techniques we can use in a situation to keep going.

This is an important area for managers:

- You can perform better if you know what helps you personally to sustain your motivation and be resilient
- You can be more effective as a manager if you know how to help your team members to persist and be resilient – using practices such as setting motivating goals, giving feedback that works, and coaching

Persistence

Persistence is the ability to keep making efforts towards a course of action, despite difficulties or opposition from others – in other words, not giving up when problems arise!

There are two important theories that underpin management practices for encouraging persistence. These are Locke and Latham's theory of goal setting[23] and Bandura's self-efficacy theory.[24]

Goal Setting

Many organisations these days use SMART or SMARTER (specific, measurable, achievable, realistic, time-bound, exciting, and rewarded) goals to direct people's efforts. Setting goals is useful in our personal lives too.

Setting goals, monitoring progress against them, and making adjustments to them are key parts of a manager's

role and are ways to ensure that everyone is pulling in the same direction and achieving the task.

We will see how to personalise goal setting for people with each of the four core motivators.

Self-Efficacy

A person's **belief** that they have the ability to do something influences how motivated they are. If they feel confident in their ability to do something, they will be motivated to do it. But if they are low in confidence, they are less likely to feel motivated and will put in less effort and be more easily discouraged when they face barriers – they will be less persistent. Confidence and self-belief are often mentioned by sports people as a factor in their success (see Chapter 5).

This means that there is a key role for managers in building their team members' ability and self-confidence.

We will look at how to develop helpful beliefs and confidence-building techniques. There are also tips on how to personalise these for different people, depending on their top motivator.

Resilience

Resilience is the ability to bounce back from the challenges and setbacks that life throws at us and maintain a positive outlook. Some people may be naturally more resilient than others, and it is believed that early experiences in life can affect how well people cope with difficulties later.

Managers can create a resilient environment for individuals and the team by role modelling and encouraging resilient habits and behaviours.

What happens to us outside work can affect our resilience and our motivation at work. This means that managers who want to enable self-motivation must be supportive towards personal problems and about issues such as work-life balance. It's also important, as a manager, to look after your own physical, mental, and emotional health, as your own behaviour has a big impact on your team members.

Take a pause here to reflect on the three elements of motivation – purpose, persistence, and resilience. What are your thoughts?

- Can you define your purpose?
- When have you shown persistence?

- What are your past experiences that you believe have increased your resilience?

Notes

THE LEADER-MANAGER'S ROLE

What does all this mean for leaders and managers?

John Kotter,[25] of Harvard Business School, made these distinctions some years ago between what a leader does and what a manager does.

Role of Leaders…	*Role of Managers…*
Coping with change	Coping with complexity
Setting direction	Planning and budgeting
Aligning people	Organising and staffing
Motivating and inspiring	Controlling and problem-solving

These days, the distinction is blurred: in practice, **most managers in organisations do a mixture of both sets of activities**, motivating and engaging people as well as monitoring and controlling. One definition of management is *getting things done through the efforts of others*. A lot is encompassed in that simple sentence! In this book I mostly refer to leader-managers.

The role of the leader-manager is not only to solve problems and make decisions so that the work gets done but also **to manage the human behaviours and relationships, the thoughts and feelings that exist in the workplace**. Leader-managers have a major impact on how people feel about their work – they are at the heart of how people experience their workplace. What the leader-manager does and says affect people's performance.

One theme that consistently emerged from my interviews with experienced managers and executives was that anyone aspiring to manage others needs to appreciate that the job of a manager of people is very different from the jobs of the people they are managing. When you become a manager, what will make you successful is completely different from what made you succeed in your previous role. This is true **as you move up the management hierarchy – different capabilities are needed at each level** and doing more of the same won't work. If you find you are trying to do the jobs of your team, then you are not working at the right level.

Managing others requires a different set of capabilities – and a positive desire to manage others. One of my interviewees[26] observed that many people managers do not enjoy managing others, so it is worth asking yourself whether managing others fits with who you are or want to be. Managing other people is not for everyone!

Successful leader-managers create the conditions in which people can find a sense of purpose in their work. They also employ people management practices effectively to enable their teams to be persistent and resilient.

Sue[27] is the Principal and CEO of a multisite College of Further Education in the UK, with thousands of students, in an area of high deprivation. In the weeks prior to the first lockdown due to COVID-19, the possibility of radical change had already been recognised as a risk, and the management team had worked together on an outline plan. When things escalated, she immediately brought together the leadership and broader management team to implement the plan over four intensive days, during which they "fully prepared for implementation to transform how we delivered learning and managed from in-person to online." Sue attributes their success to many factors, including "being crystal clear about the need to change and being very calm in creating a plan in simple steps."

As well as having this clear sense of common purpose, Sue created a team ethos. They made better decisions together, having "listened to all the different perspectives," than if she had made them alone, and governors, staff, and trade unions all contributed to this. They created a collaborative environment with a strong sense of camaraderie. She encouraged people to work across departments and to buddy up to share expertise. People started to refer to the team as their "work-family."

Sue sustained her motivation with "the thought that what we were doing was making a difference to thousands of lives." Initially, the senior team met daily and took on active, visible roles to support the managers. They also took initiatives to help students, who reside in areas classed as deprived wards, to continue their learning and address the specific challenges they faced, which included providing hundreds of laptops with training to use them effectively. There was a

> fortnightly newsletter which shared the positive things that were being done across the college, and the senior team provided the on-campus management cover for vulnerable students who remained on-site, to free up first-line managers to focus on supporting their teams.
>
> They prioritised well-being and worked on being resilient. People were encouraged to take breaks and to talk about their feelings. There was a "lockdown lounge" created for students to help with social isolation, and opportunities were made available for students and staff to support general well-being, including workshops such as online yoga and mindfulness sessions.
>
> Sue recognises that "it was all about how people felt" and that how she and the leadership team behaved had a powerful impact on that. Most of all, she says "at the heart was clear, consistent and constant communication."

Task and People

John Adair's action-centred leadership model[28] identifies three spheres of influence for the leader-manager: the task, (achieving the objective), the team (building the team), and the individuals (developing the people).

Think about the best boss you ever had. What was it that made them the best boss?

Notes

I have asked this question of teams many times, and the answers are not usually about making more profit, or cutting costs, or selling more products – they are usually the people-centred skills. People usually say that their best bosses were the ones who trusted them to get on with their work, who gave them opportunities to develop, who supported them when they needed it.

Despite this, managers often spend a lot more time on the TASK areas of their role than on the PEOPLE areas.

In the post-pandemic world, the key capabilities for managers relate to the PEOPLE areas. This doesn't mean losing sight of the

TASK but means that the focus of your attention expands towards individuals and the team. These areas of capability and action include:

ENGAGING to give meaning
DEVELOPING to build competence
DELEGATING to give freedom
CONNECTING to create belonging

As you can see, these four areas of management capability are linked to the four core needs. As a leader-manager, if you engage, develop, delegate to, and connect with your team effectively, you will tap into the core motivators of competence, freedom, belonging, and fulfilling potential (Figure 1.3).

Think about how you spend your time at work and how it divides between TASK-related activities and PEOPLE-related activities.

- Achieving the **task** includes activities such as defining the goals, identifying resources, creating a plan, establishing responsibilities, monitoring results, solving problems, and making adjustments

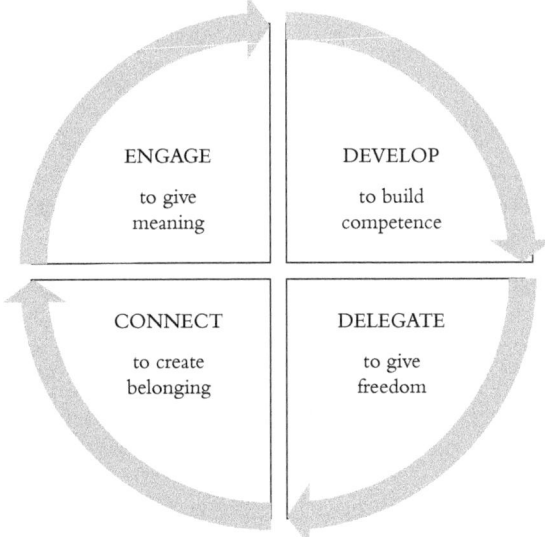

Figure 1.3 Leading Your Team to Fulfil Their Purpose and Potential

- Managing the **people** includes activities such as creating a team purpose, developing team-working, building morale, managing conflict, encouraging communication, getting to know individual's personalities, skills, and needs, and giving feedback, advice, or coaching

Try this exercise for yourself:

Think about a typical day, week, or month. Check back on your diary for the last month. What activities do you do that are related to achieving the TASK, and what activities do you do related to managing the PEOPLE? (Note, sometimes the two are intertwined – this doesn't have to be 100% accurate.)

- What proportion of your time do you typically spend in each area?
- What proportion do you think you ideally should spend in each area?

Key Activities In My Role Related To:
TASK
Actual % of time spent on TASK activities in a day or week: Ideal %:
PEOPLE
Actual % of time spent on PEOPLE activities in a day or week: Ideal %:

What is the gap between the actual proportion of time spent in each area and the ideal? How could you close the gaps?

What Activities Will You Do MORE OF or LESS OF? How Can You Make That Happen?	
More:	Less:

SUMMARY

Motivation is a combination of purpose, persistence, and resilience.

To be and stay motivated, we need:

- To have a sense of purpose which enables us to fulfil our core needs

- To have helpful thoughts and feelings that will enable us to persist
- To look after our physical, mental, and emotional needs to reduce stress and stay resilient

When these elements align, we can get into a "flow" state and be both productive and happy. Conversely, when they are out of sync, we can feel frustrated and stressed, and "not ourselves." Knowing what truly motivates you, and being able to fulfil your motivation, is the key to well-being.

Leader-managers are enablers of self-motivation. You can create the conditions for people to feel a sense of purpose and be persistent and resilient by using specific tools and techniques in four capability areas: ENGAGE to give **meaning**, DEVELOP to build **competence**, DELEGATE to give **freedom**, and CONNECT to create **belonging**. Crucially, you will also learn how to flex how you do this to meet the different needs of individuals, who have different top motivators, helping them to fulfil their potential.

ACTION PLAN

Take a pause to reflect on the key insights you have taken from this chapter and any actions you plan to take.

Insights	Actions

The first step in motivating others is to be motivated yourself. In the next chapter, you will work out which of the four core motivators is most important for you.

NOTES

1 Advice given by Philippa Perry in *The Guardian* newspaper, 17 October 2021.
2 Herzberg, F. (1968). "One More Time: How Do You Motivate Employees?" *Harvard Business Review* Vol. 46, 53–62.
3 Arnold, J., Cooper, C., and Robertson, I. (1998). *Work Psychology: Understanding Human Behaviour in the Workplace*. Harlow: Prentice Hall.
4 Csikszentmihalyi, M. (1990). "Flow: The Psychology of Optimal Experience." *Journal of Leisure Research* Vol. 24, No. 1, 93–94.

5. Amy Capstick, Head of HR for Bolton Wanderers Football Club, UK.
6. Sinek, S. (2016). *Together Is Better: A Little Book of Inspiration*. London: Penguin Books.
7. Alderfer, C. (1972). *Existence, Relatedness, and Growth: Human Needs in Organizational Settings*. New York: Free Press.
8. Maestas, N. (2010). "Back to Work: Expectations and Realisations of Work after Retirement." *Journal of Human Resources* Vol. 45, No. 3, 718–748.
9. Levitin, D. (2020). *Successful Ageing: A Neuroscientist Explores the Power and Potential of Our Lives*. Boston, MA: Dutton.
10. Danckert, J. and Eastwood, J. (2020). *Out of My Skull: The Psychology of Boredom*. Cambridge, MA: Harvard University Press.
11. Elle Hunt, article in *The Guardian* Newspaper online 4 May 2020.
12. Bishop, C. (2020). *The Long Win: The Search for a Better Way to Succeed*. Northwich: Practical Inspiration Publishing.
13. Dr Jenny Johnson, University of Liverpool Management School.
14. Lewis Pugh, interviewed by Simon Mundie, BBC Radio 4, "Don't tell me the score," October 2019.
15. Maslow, A. (1943). "A Theory of Human Motivation." *Psychological Review* Vol. 50, 370–396.
16. Ryan, R. and Deci, L. (2000). "Self-Determination Theory and the Facilitation of Intrinsic Motivation, Social Development, and Well-Being." *American Psychologist* Vol. 55, No. 1, 68–78.
17. Keirsey, D. and Bates, M. (1978). *Please Understand Me: Character and Temperament Types*. Del Mar, CA: Prometheus Nemesis.
18. Ryan, R. and Deci, L. (2000). "Self-Determination Theory and the Facilitation of Intrinsic Motivation, Social Development, and Well-Being." *American Psychologist* Vol. 55, No. 1, 68–78.
19. Berens, L. (2019). Understanding Yourself and Others™ Exploring Essential Motivators™. www.interstrength.org.
20. Keirsey, D. and Bates, M. (1978). *Please Understand Me: Character and Temperament Types*. Del Mar, CA: Prometheus Nemesis.
21. Lewis Pugh, interviewed by Simon Mundie, BBC Radio 4, "Don't tell me the score," October 2019.
22. Max Whitlock, interviewed by Simon Mundie, BBC Radio 4, "Don't tell me the score," March 2020.
23. Locke, E. and Latham, G. (1990). "A Theory of Goal Setting & Task Performance." *The Academy of Management Review* Vol. 16, No. 2, 480–483.
24. Bandura, A. (1977). "Self-efficacy: Toward a Unifying Theory of Behavioral Change." *Psychological Review* Vol. 84, No. 2, 191–215.
25. Kotter, J. P. (1990). *A Force for Change: How Leadership Differs from Management*. New York: Free Press.
26. Helen Bradley, Client Director, Executive Education, Imperial College Business School.
27. Sue Higginson, Principal and CEO of Wirral Metropolitan College.
28. Adair, J. (1973). *Action-Centred Leadership*. New York: McGraw-Hill.

WHAT'S YOUR PURPOSE? – HOW TO FIND YOUR "WHY"

INTRODUCTION

Motivating others starts with motivating yourself. Your own top motivator has a big impact on how you lead others. In this chapter, you will assess which of the four core motivators is strongest for you.

Through self-insight activities, a quiz, and case studies, you will explore:

- Your signature strengths and talents
- Your interests and values
- How you behave in many different situations over time – not just about what you did yesterday or how you feel today

You may want to ask other people who know you well for their opinions. Sometimes we take our talents for granted and don't realise they are special, because we assume everyone has them. Yet our talents are usually linked to what motivates us.

Through the activities and exercises you will build up a picture of yourself:

- Who are you really?
- What makes you feel fulfilled?
- Why do you choose to do some things rather than others?
- What do you get out of them?

There is perhaps nothing worse than reaching the top of the ladder and discovering that you're on the wrong wall.[1] *Joseph Campbell*

Doing the exercises will give you an anchor of self-insight before you consider how to enable self-motivation in others. It will enhance the value you get from the book, both for yourself personally and in appreciating other types of motivation.

By the end of the chapter, you should have made an estimate of which of the four core motivators fits you best. You will find out what gives you a sense of purpose and meaning and drives your behaviour. Some of the activities will relate to your life outside work as well as in work. While this book is primarily about motivation at work, sometimes what you choose to do outside work illuminates your understanding of what it is that truly motivates you.

You can take questionnaires to find out what motivates you, and there is one later in this chapter. There are also free ones available on the internet (see Appendix for recommended ones). But no questionnaire can be relied upon to be completely accurate. All questionnaires have measurement error. And we often fill them in based on what has recently happened, so they are skewed to things that are on our minds now, while the core motivators are about patterns of behaviour over long periods of time. As well as questionnaires, you can use other ways to find out about yourself which together can form a more accurate picture. Here is one to start with.

SELF-INSIGHT ACTIVITY 1

Think about how you spend your time at work. List your main activities – what you do in a typical day or week – on a separate sheet of paper, and then fill them in on a table like the one below, in the correct boxes, depending on how much you enjoy them and how well you believe you do them.

The table includes notes made by a senior leader (Louis) as an example.

	Enjoy	*Don't Enjoy*
Do well	*Talents – plan to do more?* Coaching the members of my team and seeing them develop	*Plan to reduce or change?* Making presentations to senior people when I don't know all the detail

| Don't do well | *Potential strengths – plan to develop?*

Discussing with clients what they need from my team | *Plan to fix!*

Being asked to devise strategic plans with no guidance on where to start or what is required |

When Louis completed his chart, he realised that working with and helping other people made him feel valued and motivated and that these were elements he could do more of and would want in any future role. He recognised that as he became more senior, he would need to be comfortable without knowing all the detail. He also realised that thinking about long-term strategy did not come naturally to him and that it would make sense to delegate it or work collaboratively on it.

Use the chart for yourself, to start to explore some of your talents.

	Enjoy	*Don't Enjoy*
Do well	*Talents – plan to do more?*	*Plan to reduce or change?*
Don't do well	*Potential strengths – plan to develop?*	*Plan to fix!*

This activity helps you become more aware of your talents and potential strengths. People usually find roles more satisfying when they can use their interests in carrying out that role; they find roles where they are not able to use their interests dissatisfying. What does this activity suggest about your interests? For example:

- Do you prefer roles where you spend a lot of time with others or more time alone?
- Do you like realistic, practical activities, or do you prefer imaginative and creative ones?
- Are you more interested in helping people or in achieving tasks?
- Do you like to organise and structure your time, or do you prefer to respond to what happens?

Make a note of anything that stands out for you. What do you find satisfying or dissatisfying? What interests you?

My Interests

SELF-INSIGHT ACTIVITY 2

In activity 1, you looked at where you are now – your role, what you enjoy or not, what you do well or not, and what you find satisfying or dissatisfying.

In this activity, think about your past life and all the things that you are proud of and for which you feel a sense of achievement, both inside and outside work. These can be small things as well as big things – it doesn't matter whether other people would think they were achievements. It is what *you* are proud of that matters. List all your positive accomplishments and successes of the past. Some examples are included to start you off.

My Achievements
E.g. playing in the school football team, winning a prize for art, working hard to pass an exam, getting a job with a charity, designing a new product, running a marathon to fundraise, building a shed, getting promoted…

Now think about what personal strengths you drew on to achieve those things. It might help you to talk this over with someone. Write these strengths in the box below.

My Strengths
E.g. determination, creativity, empathy, numeracy, caring about others, practical skills…

Spend a few moments to consider how far you are using these strengths currently. Sometimes we have budding strengths and talents when we are young, but in adulthood they can become swamped by the pressures of daily life, work, family, and so on. We put aside what interests us to meet external demands, and we neglect our talents.

Consider what factors might be stopping you using your strengths in your daily life. What are the ways you might be blocking yourself? What are the barriers to using your strengths?

Barriers and Blocks to Using My Strengths
E.g. no opportunity to use the strength in my current role, too many other things to do, giving up when people criticise my ideas, lack of self-confidence, impostor syndrome, fear of failure…

SELF-INSIGHT ACTIVITY 3

The final self-insight activity takes you into an imaginary future. Here are some questions for you.

	Question: If you won the lottery…	Answer
1.	What would you change in your life?	
2.	What would you do with your time?	
3.	What appeals to you about that?	
4.	What would you do in a typical day?	
5.	What would a typical week look like?	
6.	What would be the highlight of your year?	
7.	What do your answers tell you about your interests and values?	

The activity above is to help you reflect on what is important to you – your values. Many people say that their family is the most important thing in their life, and this is true for sure. They are at the top of your priority list, but what comes second? What else makes you feel good about yourself? What would you really like to do if you had a free choice? And what would that give you?

Here are some values to prompt your thinking. Tick the five that are most important to you now, or add ones of your own.

Achievement	Truth	Learning	Reliability	Efficiency
Autonomy	Fairness	Fun	Respect	Enthusiasm
Creativity	Justice	Competence	Initiative	Generosity
Belonging	Security	Adventure	Integrity	Health
Harmony	Responsibility	Ambition	Friendship	Personal growth
Honesty	Duty	Caring	Status	Wisdom
Openness	Freedom	Wealth	Adaptability	Risk-taking
Excellence	Forgiveness	Environment	Independence	Trust

What do your top five values tell you about what motivates you?

My Values

SUMMARY SO FAR

Now that you have done the three self-insight activities, you will see some themes emerging.

Capture your thoughts now before we move on. What are your signature strengths and talents (i.e. what do you do best)? What are your interests and values (i.e. what really matters to you)?

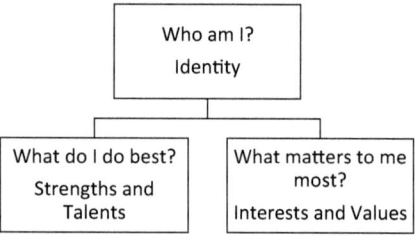

Strengths	Talents	Interests	Values

QUIZ

Now that you have done the self-insight activities, try this quiz. It will help you identify your patterns of behaviour, which are linked to the four core motivators.

Answers to personality quizzes are not always accurate indicators of the real you, but your answers to this quiz will add to the picture you are building up of yourself. It will help you decide which of the four core motivators fits you best. After completing it, look at your results alongside your conclusions from the three self-insight activities.

You can also download this quiz from www.essenwood.co.uk.

The quiz is in three parts. Start with Part 1. Depending on your answers to Part 1, you will go on either to Part 2A or to Part 2B.

Part 1

For each question, tick the option (A or B) that you believe best describes your usual approach — if you really can't decide, leave it blank. Think about how you are when you are being "yourself," probably at home, rather than how you might be forced to be by circumstances or by your work.

Please be honest — you do not have to share this with anyone!

1.	My favourite tasks	
	A. Are practical and produce tangible results	
	B. Involve imagination and innovation to solve the problem	
2.	I prefer other people to see me as	
	A. Realistic and practical	
	B. Imaginative and creative	
3.	After I've watched a film, I am more likely to remember	
	A. The action – what happened	
	B. The theme – what it was about	
4.	When I make a suggestion, I tend to	
	A. Start with the details to ensure clarity	
	B. Give an overview first and then maybe add details	
5.	I tend to be more interested in	
	A. Facts and details in the present, or remembered from the past	
	B. Ideas and possibilities	

6.	When I am in conversation, I tend to	
	A. Talk in factual terms and stick to the topic at hand	
	B. Use metaphors or make connections that expand the topic	
7.	When I look at a painting, I tend to	
	A. Notice the details – people, objects, colours, layout	
	B. Wonder what it means or what the artist intended	
8.	When I'm with friends, I prefer to	
	A. Talk about everyday reality – home, work, news – "what is"	
	B. Talk about what everyday reality means – patterns, ideas, and the future – "what might be"	
9	When I'm learning something new, I prefer to learn something	
	A. That's practical and useful right now	
	B. That expands my mind or captures my imagination	
10.	I most like to be appreciated for	
	A. My practical outputs	
	B. My helpful ideas and insights	
11.	When my boss asks for an update on my work, I like to give	
	A. Detailed and factual information on what I am doing	
	B. A broad overview about how my work is going	
12.	When observing something or someone, it's natural for me to	
	A. Notice all the details of what is there in the moment	
	B. Read between the lines and see hidden patterns and meanings	
13.	I am more likely to be described by others as	
	A. Being "down to earth"	
	B. Having my "head in the clouds"	

Count how many ticks you have for options A and B and record the number here:

Number of questions answered with option A: _____

Number of questions answered with option B: _____

Write which answer (A or B) you chose more often here: _____

Now, if you chose A, **go on to Part 2A**. If you chose B, **go on to Part 2B**.

Part 2A

This part of the quiz is for people who came out with more A answers in Part 1.

For each question, tick the option (A or B) that you believe best describes your usual approach – if you really can't decide, leave it blank. Think about how you are when you are being "yourself," probably at home, rather than how you might be forced to be by circumstances or by your work.

1.	When a decision is needed,	
	A. I prefer it when things are completely settled	
	B. I sometimes keep it open so I can respond to what happens	
2.	If something comes up unexpectedly at work, which needs my attention	
	A. I prefer to finish what I had already intended to do first	
	B. I prefer to take a look at the new issue straight away	
3.	After I've made a decision, if new information comes in	
	A. I feel irritated at having to reopen the decision	
	B. I feel comfortable revisiting the decision	
4.	When planning a day out	
	A. I like to know exactly what we are going to do	
	B. I like to have a general idea which we can adapt as we go along	
5.	When a change is proposed, my first reaction is often	
	A. If it's not broken, don't fix it	
	B. What can I do to get started on it	
6.	When I have a new project at work	
	A. I feel tense until I can make a start on it	
	B. I feel excited before making a start on it	
7.	I use to-do lists as a way of	
	A. Keeping track of what I must do	
	B. Remembering what I might do	
8.	I meet my deadlines by	
	A. Starting early and always working steadily towards the deadline	
	B. Perhaps starting early and always relying on a burst of energy as the deadline approaches	

9	When an important decision has to be made	
	A. I like to get the decision made as soon as possible	
	B. I often feel pressured to make it sooner than it needs to be made	
10.	When I have a plan	
	A. I stick to the plan and only change it if absolutely necessary	
	B. I am happy to alter the plan if new information or a better idea comes up	
11.	At weekends, I can	
	A. Relax after I have finished the jobs I need to do	
	B. Relax and enjoy myself even when there are jobs to do	
12.	Before starting something new, I prefer to	
	A. Work out a plan with specific steps and deadlines	
	B. Start on the task and let the plan emerge	
13.	When I am in a difficult situation, I tend to first	
	A. Think back to a similar situation I experienced previously	
	B. See options for dealing with it in the moment	

Count how many ticks you have for options A and B and record the number here:

Number of questions answered with option A: _____

Number of questions answered with option B: _____

Write which answer (A or B) you chose more often here: _____

Now skip Part 2B, and go on to the end of the quiz to find out which top motivator correlates with the choices you have made.

Part 2B

This part of the quiz is for people who came out with more B answers in Part 1.

For each question, tick the option (A or B) that you believe best describes your usual approach – if you really can't decide, leave it blank. Think about how you are when you are being "yourself," probably at home, rather than how you might be forced to be by circumstances or by your work.

1.	When I make a decision, I like to first	
	A. Identify the relevant factors, considering each as objectively as possible	
	B. Consider how it will impact each of the people or groups involved	
2.	I mostly like to receive positive feedback for	
	A. Situations where I'm confident in the quality of the work I have produced	
	B. The personal effort and emotional commitment I have put in	
3.	When debating ideas with others, it's important to	
	A. Get to the truth, even at the cost of harmony	
	B. Have harmony even at the cost of the whole truth	
4.	When I have a decision to make, I first of all carefully consider	
	A. What objective principles and criteria I will apply	
	B. How other people will be affected	
5.	I most value my ability to be	
	A. Objective under pressure	
	B. Empathetic under pressure	
6.	When I review other people's work, it comes naturally to me to	
	A. Critique and suggest improvements	
	B. Appreciate and give praise	
7.	When I discuss ideas with others, I ask questions to first	
	A. Understand what they think	
	B. Find out how they are feeling	
8.	I help friends to solve their problems by	
	A. Helping them define their problem and then find solutions	
	B. Showing sympathy and concern and checking how they feel	
9.	I tend to prioritise	
	A. Achieving my goals while still not forgetting connecting with others	
	B. Connecting with others while still not forgetting achieving my goals	
10.	When someone criticises my ideas	
	A. I tend not to take it personally	
	B. My feelings are easily hurt	

11.	All things being equal, I prefer a tutor who	
	A. Is expert and confident	
	B. I feel a good bond with	
12.	When a friend is upset about something,	
	A. I understand how they must be feeling	
	B. I share their feelings of upset	
13.	When a change is proposed, I like to	
	A. Understand the reasons why	
	B. Know how it will affect people	

Count how many ticks you have for options A and B and record the number here:

Number of questions answered with option A: _____

Number of questions answered with option B: _____

Write which answer (A or B) you chose more often here: _____

Now find out which motivation pattern correlates with the choices you have made.

Quiz Results

You should now have **one** of these four combinations of preferences. Tick which one applies to you.

- AA or AB or BA or BB

Each of these correlates with one of the four core motivators and patterns of behaviour.

- AA – Need for Belonging – Stabiliser
- AB – Need for Freedom – Improviser
- BA – Need for Competence – Theorist
- BB – Need to Fulfil Potential – Catalyst

This grouping of behaviours, based on temperament theory, has stood the test of time and gives us awareness and meaningful insights, but it will not explain everything about you. It is consistent with self-determination theory, as noted in Chapter 1.

People usually identify clearly with one pattern, but sometimes they recognise some aspects of themselves in one or two of the others, and this is perfectly normal. These are not hard and fast categories – they group people with similar motivations and patterns of behaviour together, but each of us is much more complex than any single model of personality can describe. As we mature, we expand out from our core to take on other perspectives and become more rounded and balanced human beings.

DECISION TIME!

You now have the self-insight activities and the quiz to help you assess which of the four core motivators and patterns of behaviour fits you best. Before deciding, read the four sets of statements below – which is most important to you? You might relate to all these things, and of course, that is true up to a point. But if you had to rank them in order of importance to you – what must you absolutely have in your work to be happy and fulfilled – which of these four groupings would come top of your ranking? Put them in rank order. If it seems difficult to choose, start by eliminating the one that is least important to you.

- FREEDOM: do you want the freedom to act and get impressive quick results? – the IMPROVISER pattern. Do you like to:

  - Be noticed
  - Make an immediate concrete impact
  - Have freedom to act
  - Get impressive quick results

- BELONGING: do you want to do your duty for the group and be responsible? – the STABILISER pattern. Do you like to:

  - Be responsible
  - Contribute to the group
  - Have structure and consistency
  - Respect tradition and continuity

- COMPETENCE: do you want to reach mastery and contribute to progress? – the THEORIST pattern. Do you like to:

  - Be competent
  - Bring knowledge and expertise
  - Have intellectual independence
  - Contribute to progress

- POTENTIAL: do you want to be true to yourself and help others be the best they can be? – the CATALYST pattern. Do you like to:

  - Be authentic
  - Make a difference to others and the world
  - Have purpose and meaning
  - Fulfil potential

Credit to Linda Berens and Susan Nash.

What especially fits you about the pattern you have selected? How do you express this pattern of behaviour in your work? Which elements of other patterns also fit you?

Notes

Now look back to the summary you did earlier in this chapter before the quiz, about your strengths, talents, interests, and values. How well do they fit with the core motivator and pattern of behaviour you have selected?

- How do you use your strengths and talents to fulfil your core motivator?
- How do your interests and values link to your core motivator?

Notes

If your strengths, talents, interests, and values do not seem to fit the pattern of behaviour that you selected here, or how you scored on the quiz, then maybe another pattern would fit you better. You can explore this further in the next chapter where you will find the typical characteristics of people with all four patterns.

Remember that people with different patterns can be motivated by different aspects of the same role. Here is an example of four website designers, who have different patterns, yet are all successful in the same role.

> *Sook Yee* has the Improviser (freedom) behaviour pattern. What really motivates her as a website designer is solving immediate problems. She feels energised when a client's website needs urgent work, and she leaps into action to diagnose the problem and implement solutions. She loves the kudos she gets for being able to handle a crisis. She also feels satisfied when websites are dynamic, colourful, and visually appealing. She is not so keen on the routine work of maintaining her clients' websites.
>
> *James* has the Stabiliser (belonging) behaviour pattern. He likes designing websites, using tried and tested methods. He enjoys working alongside his client as part of the team, and he feels satisfied when his websites are rated by them as fit for purpose, practical, and user-friendly. He does not enjoy dealing with a crisis, but if he must, he goes about it in an orderly, methodical way.
>
> *Sarah* has the Theorist (competence) behaviour pattern. She feels motivated when she is given a new design project, and she is energised to produce something new for each client rather than adapt what has been done before. She likes to be regarded as an expert by her clients and is pleased when they come to her for advice. She feels satisfied when her websites are interesting, show an intelligent approach, and are effective.
>
> *Rohan* has the Catalyst (potential) behaviour pattern. He really likes getting to know his clients and feel that he is helping them to achieve worthwhile goals that will make a real difference to their business. He always takes time to build a personal connection with them, and he is satisfied when he feels he has a special relationship with them. He likes to feel that they value him for who he is, as well as for the work he does.

You can see from these case studies that we look for different things in a role, and it is possible to tap into and fulfil different needs from the same situation.

If you are unsure which core motivator and pattern of behaviour fits you best, you can continue to explore by reading the next chapter, which sets out the characteristics of each core motivator and behaviour pattern in more detail and what they mean for the way you like to work.

SUMMARY

There are many things that can potentially give us a sense of purpose, something that is meaningful to us and moves us to action.

In addition, we have psychological needs for competence, freedom, belonging, and fulfilling potential. We usually rank one of these needs above the others, but they all have some importance.

The aim of the three self-insight activities and the quiz was to give you a range of different ways to discover your core needs and motivators. These needs are expressed through your personality and patterns of behaviour and are grouped into four categories summarised by the terms:

- Freedom – Improviser
- Competence – Theorist
- Belonging – Stabiliser
- Potential – Catalyst

They are not hard and fast categories – they are groupings of people who share similar characteristics but will also have many individual differences.

Being aware of what most motivates you means you can play to your strengths and make choices about your career that fit with your interests and values. You can also appreciate that others may be motivated differently and therefore how you might need to flex your leadership style to enable their self-motivation.

ACTION PLAN

Take a pause to reflect on the key insights you have taken from this chapter and any actions you plan to take.

Insights	Actions

The next chapter describes the impact of the different core motivators on how people behave at work.

NOTE

1 Campbell, J. (2014). *The Hero's Journey: Joseph Campbell on His Life and Work*. Novato, CA: New World Library.

ONE SIZE DOESN'T FIT ALL – THE FOUR CORE MOTIVATORS

INTRODUCTION

Each of the four core motivators drives us to behave in certain ways, and these become recognisable parts of our personality. This does not mean that behaviour is always predictable – we can flex behaviour depending on the situation, and we change and mature over time. How we behave is also influenced by our upbringing, education, experiences, the culture in which we live, our circumstances, and the work we do.

But we do have underlying core motivations and patterns of behaviour that endure over time. Grouping people who share certain characteristics together helps us make sense of ourselves and of them while recognising that we also have many individual differences.

This chapter describes the patterns of behaviour that are linked to each of the four core motivators. You will learn more about your own motivation and behaviour **and** be more aware of the impact of different motivators on the behaviour and performance of your team members.

There are practical examples of how the four core motivators are expressed and their impact on how people behave at work:

- Their likely talents and strengths
- The challenges they may face
- What is likely to energise them in a job and career
- Their communication style

Meaningful work isn't about impressing others. It's about expressing your values. *Adam Grant*[1]

DOI: 10.4324/9781003286646-4

THE IMPROVISER MOTIVATION PATTERN

Figure 3.1 The Improviser Motivation

Their Inner Drive

At the core of the Improviser motivation pattern – why they do what they do – is the need to have autonomy and **freedom** to act. They want to be noticed and to make an immediate concrete impact. They like to deal swiftly with whatever comes up and get impressive quick results.

The animal metaphor for this motivation pattern is the fox (Figure 3.1).[2] Foxes are resourceful and adaptable, quick thinking and fast acting. They are very attuned to their environment, able to spot, and take any opportunities that arise. They look sleek and well-groomed. They seem to move in a smooth and coordinated fashion. These characteristics represent the Improviser's desire to have an impact and be impressive in the moment.

Talents and Strengths

People with the Improviser motivation pattern are often described by others using words such as:

Practical	Flexible	Bold	Animated
Adaptable	Impulsive	Daring	Spontaneous
Risk-taking	Attention-seeking	Adventurous	Fun

Easily bored	Generous	Factual	Rebellious
Entertainer	Kind	Realistic	Restless
Casual	Sensitive	Optimistic	Playful

They pay attention to the present and focus on exactly what is happening right here and right now. They can take in and analyse information on the spot, including what other people are saying and doing. They are realistic, and they jump quickly into action – if an approach doesn't work, they will rapidly try something else instead.

Improvisers can act in the moment and take quick decisions, and this means that they can be excellent in a crisis. In fact, people with this motivation pattern usually enjoy handling a crisis – they feel energised and effective and are comfortable being at the centre of the action. Helen Mirren (British actress), Paul Merton (British comedian), and Joe Wicks (British fitness coach who during the coronavirus epidemic in 2020 gave daily workouts on YouTube) present themselves in a way which indicates an Improviser/Freedom motivation.

People with the Improviser pattern tend to pay attention to and trust what they experience with their senses, in the present moment. They notice small details and cues in the people and things around them. They trust what is real and concrete, things that can be measured and counted. They tend to doubt insights and things that can't be proved.

Their unique talent is their tactical skills. They are confident trouble-shooters and natural negotiators. They see themselves parachuting in to resolve problems and get things moving.

They like to be recognised for *how* they work and contribute.[3] Their favourite question at work is *"what can I do now?"*.

Will and Chantal both found roles that enabled them to use their Improviser talents to the full – particularly their liking for immediate concrete experience and their practical resourcefulness.

Will left school without qualifications and went into the army. When he left the army, he got a job in car sales and progressed rapidly to become the head of a retail site of a luxury car brand. He is adept at interpreting data, understanding the key business metrics

(Continued)

and getting to the nub of commercial issues. He is *quick witted* and able to *think on his feet* when challenged by his bosses or when negotiating with customers, and he can *do a deal rapidly*. He likes the *physical environment* of the showroom, being surrounded by luxury cars, and he *enjoys being seen* driving them. He gets frustrated with long meetings and interminable discussions – he wants to get on and DO something. He does not like to be managed or monitored by his boss – he wants the *freedom to run the business* in his own way.

Chantal is an estate agent. She loves having lots of interaction with her clients, both the buyers and the sellers. She enjoys *being out and about*, visiting properties and their owners and meeting buyers and doing viewings. She is sensitive to how people respond to a property, and this helps her decide how to "sell" to them. No two days are the same, and she likes having *a flexible, relatively unstructured schedule*. She previously worked in fashion retail and has a *good eye for how things look* – she uses this flair when she evaluates properties, and she advises her clients on how best to present them.

Challenges

The challenges for people with the Improviser motivation are the downsides of their strengths:

- They tend not to like following routines and procedures
- They quickly become bored when discussions take too long
- They may become impatient with people who want to check and control their activity
- They may jump to action too quickly and not consider all the options or wider implications
- They can appear to make things up on the hoof which can be stressful for others
- They tend to meet deadlines at the last minute, rather than in advance
- They may put off making decisions until it becomes urgent

> *Jess* is a lecturer in a college. She loves being among her students and sees herself as *a "performer."* She is always ready with a witty riposte to defuse any poor behaviour. She likes to *do her own thing*, and she usually finds ways to deal with admin and procedures as quickly as possible. Her *unwillingness to follow rules imposed by others* was illustrated when she told me that at home, when emptying the dishwasher, her partner likes the cutlery to be put away with forks, knives, and spoons in separate sections in the drawer. She feels this is unnecessary, so when she empties the dishwasher, she tips all the cutlery into the drawer randomly. She didn't tell me how her partner feels about this!
>
> *Hamid* was a manager in a water utility company whose colleague, *Dave*, managed the adjacent area, and they needed to follow common processes and approaches across the whole region. Hamid was motivated by a need *to belong and contribute to the team*, and his style was to be *organised and proceed step by step*, typical of the Stabiliser motivation pattern. He constantly clashed with Dave, who was *good at dealing with a crisis, liked immediate action, and was impatient with processes* – typical of the Improviser motivation pattern. Hamid felt undermined because his core needs to *do his duty to the wider team* were not respected by Dave. Similarly, Dave felt undermined because his need for the *freedom to act* and be *impressive in dealing with a crisis* was not valued by Hamid. There were constant problems in the team, and their relationship had become so poor that they could only see the negative side of each other's behaviour and not the underlying talents.

What Improvisers Need in a Job

What is key when choosing a career is to be aware of your core needs and look for jobs that will provide *enough* opportunity to fulfil those needs *in an environment that feels right for you*. When you can tap into your core motivation in your work, you are more likely to experience being in "flow."[4] People with the Improviser motivation pattern are often attracted to active, physical work (Figure 3.2).

Figure 3.2 Improvisers at Work

They flourish in jobs where they can:

- Use their tactical skills, troubleshoot, and sort out problems in the moment
- Be hands-on, practical, and get concrete results
- Do active, physical work or be out and about
- Deal with data and information that relate to things in the real world
- Be appreciated for getting things done
- Work in a role where there is flexibility, variety, and fun and not too many meetings or schedules to follow
- Work in a business or service organisation where they can deal with real and concrete things or help other people in a hands-on, practical way
- Get immediate feedback from seeing their results
- Focus on experience in the present rather than planning for the future

> When I first met **Baki**, he told me that one of the best jobs he ever had was as an entertainer on a cruise ship. He loved being the centre of attention, and getting the ***immediate feedback*** from his audience, being able to see that they liked him and his performance.
>
> He became the head of a retail site for a luxury car brand. Like Will (above), he was very ***attuned to what was going on around him*** – he was always aware of who was in the showroom, of new customers walking in, of what his team were doing. He chose to have an office on the ground floor (rather than in the "management suite" upstairs), where he could ***be on the spot***.
>
> He ***enjoyed negotiating*** with customers, and he also liked the league table ***competition*** with the other sites in their franchise. The ***incentives and prizes*** available in the retail motor trade motivated him.

Not everyone with the Improviser pattern likes to be the centre of attention. Baki was a more extraverted personality and enjoyed interacting with others to deal with practical issues on the spot. More introverted people tend to prefer less interaction with others, but they share the core motivations of needing freedom and flexibility and being hands-on with real and concrete activities.

> **Becky** has the Improviser motivation and is typically ***adaptable and flexible***. She has enjoyed different jobs over the years – teaching young children where she brought ***spontaneity and fun***, doing clerical work for a hospice where she helped to meet people's emotional needs, and working on the tills in a garden centre where she ***provided practical help to people*** to make their gardens more attractive. The common theme in all these jobs was ***serving other people in a tangible way and doing practical work that has an impact***.

Communication Style

Improvisers tend to have a casual, informal style of communication. They do not stand on ceremony and may be seen at work – particularly in organisations that have a lot of rules and procedures – as a little disruptive.

They usually talk about concrete, real-world things – the news, sport, the weather, family, work, facts and figures, who is doing what and what is happening when, and local events.

They tend to be quite brief in their communication. They use a lot of action words and words such as "fun," "excitement," and "challenge." They tend to ask questions beginning with "What" and "How." They focus on the present rather than the past or future. They mention details, facts, and figures, and they give or ask for evidence. They often use humour and tell anecdotes – they can be great raconteurs. They often dress to impress – they like to look good and have an impact.

Their written communication also tends to be concise and specific. They do not pay a lot of attention to long, written documents, preferring to get to the point without needing to know a lot of information or explanation. This can mean that they may miss or forget important information. They often have a good memory for physical activities and movement.

Sometimes they can appear to their colleagues as unprepared, but their ability to respond quickly in the moment usually means they get away with it!

THE STABILISER MOTIVATION PATTERN

Their Inner Drive

At the core of the Stabiliser motivation pattern – why they do what they do – is a need for relatedness and **belonging**. They want be

"I enjoy working with others to get practical durable results"

Figure 3.3 The Stabiliser Motivation

part of a group and do their duty to it. They are naturally responsible, and they respect tradition and like to have structure and consistency.

The animal metaphor for this motivation pattern is the Beaver (Figure 3.3). Beavers are hard-working animals who cut down vegetation to construct dams and build lodges for their families. If you have ever been near beavers at dusk, you may not see them, but you will hear them chomping away at the undergrowth to maintain and reinforce their homes. These characteristics of working hard to protect your family or to create firm foundations, acting to reduce risks, and wanting to belong to a community are typical of people with the Stabiliser motivation pattern.

Talents and Strengths

People with this pattern are often described by others as:

Reliable	Persistent	Trustworthy	Organised
Consistent	Traditional	Modest	Methodical
Straightforward	Conventional	Humble	Altruistic
Conscientious	Helpful	Concerned	Respectable
Dutiful	Kind	Realistic	Careful
Responsible	Dependable	Practical	Steadfast
Safety conscious	Results-oriented	Diligent	Busy

They are dependable – if you want something done, it's a good idea to ask someone with the Stabiliser motivation pattern to do it. They get their sense of purpose from contributing to the group and feeling they belong. This could be groups at work, their family, their neighbourhood, their religious group, or other social or hobby groups.

They enjoy being of service to others and feel energised when they are actively carrying out tasks that help other people or their community. They have a strong sense of duty, and they value tradition. Mother Teresa and David Beckham probably shared this motivation.

People with the Stabiliser pattern tend to pay attention to and trust what is real and concrete, things that can be measured and counted. They draw on past experience to guide their action. They rely on what they already know, and they usually have very good memories for specific practical things and for information they have recorded in their minds for future use. They tend to doubt insights and things that can't be proved with solid evidence.

Their unique talent is their logistical skills – getting everything to the right place at the right time. They may see themselves as a cog in a machine keeping their part ticking over and contributing to the bigger machine.

They like to be recognised for *what* they produce, the results of their efforts.[5] Their favourite question at work might be *"what are the boundaries?"*.

> When **Ben** retired from work, he knew that he wanted to volunteer his skills towards something worthwhile. He became a Trustee of some charities in areas in which he had an interest. As well as getting satisfaction from knowing he was ***helping a good cause***, it was important to him to feel ***part of a team***, to connect with the other people involved in running the charities and to do ***practical things to further their objectives***. He also got involved in running other voluntary organisations in his community – the sports club of which he was a member and the local village traffic committee. Like most people with the Stabiliser motivation pattern, Ben felt most himself when he was able to ***do practical things in an organised structure*** that was working to keep things running efficiently.

People with the Stabiliser pattern usually like consistency and predictability, so having rules, procedures, and processes to follow makes sense to them. They apply their logistical skills to organising events and projects.

> *Flavia* is a senior manager in a technical organisation who has the Stabiliser motivation pattern. When she came to me for coaching, she told me that she loved helping people. She has a reputation for being ***reliable and getting things done***, and people often come to her for assistance. She ***drops what she is doing to help them***, and it makes her feel good that ***she is needed and trusted***. Outside work, she often spends her weekends and spare time ***helping her friends and neighbours with practical projects***. She likes the feeling of ***being relied on*** and that they value her contribution – it makes her feel that ***she belongs***.

Challenges

When people with the Stabiliser pattern see that something needs to be done, they will often step in to do it, even when it is not their responsibility. This can sometimes lead them to overburden themselves. Pitfalls include:

- They tend to take on too much themselves
- They may have difficulty with saying no
- They tend to pick up tasks instead of letting others take responsibility
- They can be perceived as inflexible
- They may regard time spent discussing ideas and possibilities as pointless
- They may struggle to see ways to deal with new problems
- They may make decisions quickly before considering all the options and possibilities
- They may become exhausted but not think through how to change the situation

> **Luke** realises that at times his need to help others stops him from *fulfilling his responsibilities* in his own job, particularly those aspects that are longer term and don't have an immediate deadline. He is always busy but knows that he isn't always busy on the right things for the organisation. He finds this dilemma stressful. In coaching we worked on how he could change his mindset to feel ok about ring-fencing time for his own priorities and to think of this as a contribution to the team, rather than feeling that he was letting people down when he couldn't help them.

Tensions can arise at work between people with different motivation patterns. In the Improviser section, we saw the case of Hamid and Dave, where Hamid had the Stabiliser temperament. Here is an example of the Stabiliser and Theorist motivations leading to conflict.

> ***Jonny*** was a team leader, and he sometimes ran into conflict with one of his team members. Jonny was very ***organised*** in his approach to work and was always ***on top of his tasks*** – typical of the Stabiliser motivation pattern. When his manager asked him to do something, he always dealt with it straightaway. He expected others to do the same. But he found it frustrating that one of his team members, ***Charlie***, did not act on his requests immediately. Charlie, who had the Theorist motivation pattern, would carry on with ***her own priorities*** and fit in Jonny's request when she felt it was necessary. She was irritated when he chased her up before she had done the task. She had a core need to be ***independent and in control of her work*** – she liked to ***make her own decisions*** on the relative importance of what Jonny had asked her to do. This annoyed Jonny, as he interpreted this as a sign that she did not respect him, which was not the case – she just wanted to stick to ***the logic of her own priorities***. The underlying conflict was resolved when Jonny was coached to agree a deadline for tasks that he delegated and not to chase them up until the deadline arrived.

What They Need in a Job

People with the Stabiliser motivation pattern have a strong sense of duty and are often attracted to business or service industries (Figure 3.4).

They will flourish in jobs where they can:

- Use their logistical skills
- Be part of a team
- Follow accepted ways of doing things and proven procedures
- Work in a cooperative atmosphere with other conscientious people
- Have clear decisions and follow plans in a consistent way
- Work in a role where they can achieve practical results and tangible outputs (often in business or service industries)
- Work in an organisation which has clear lines of authority and an orderly rather than chaotic atmosphere
- Use their experience from the past
- Live up to their perceived responsibilities
- Focus on real and concrete things, sometimes comparing present data with past experiences

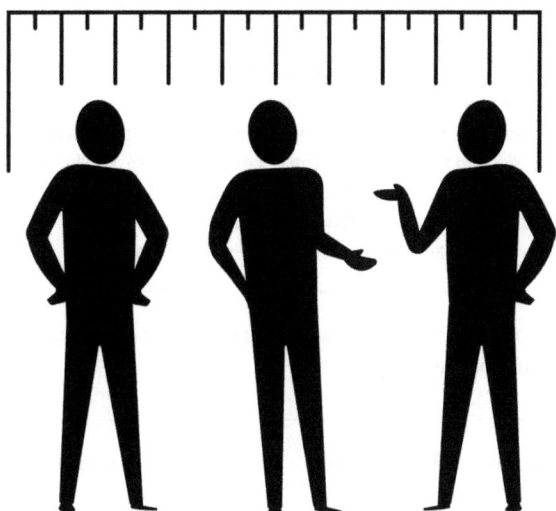

Figure 3.4 Stabilisers at Work

> **Donna** has the Stabiliser motivation pattern and she manages the administrative staff within a college. She enjoys being in a ***position of authority*** and is comfortable ***giving direction and making decisions***. The admin functions have a reputation for "running like clockwork," and this is largely due to the way she manages the team, with an emphasis on ***following established procedures***. For several years in a row, they have won the annual "best support department" award, and she is very ***proud of her team*** and their contribution to the success of the college.

There are differences in how the Stabiliser motivation pattern is expressed, depending on whether the person is more extraverted or more introverted. The primary difference is that the more extraverted tend to like to work in a busy atmosphere with other people, while the more introverted tend to be comfortable working in one-to-one situations or alone for parts of the day.

> *Ayesha* is more introverted. She works in an accounting department and is very accurate and *methodical* in her work. She has strong powers of concentration and can work alone for long periods. She likes *working to a schedule* to produce the accounts and feels a sense of achievement when they are completed on time and with no errors. She feels good that she is able to use her skills *in the service of* the Accounting team and likes to *feel part of a team*, but she does not need to have constant interaction with them. She has an *orderly working environment*, with everything she needs, including her physical and digital files, in the right place.

A strength for people with the Stabiliser pattern is being able to draw on their memory of past experience.

> *Ayesha* (above) has a reputation in the office for being able to remember things. Whenever a problem crops up, she can *recall* how similar problems have been dealt with in the past, and she draws on that experience to help work out what to do. When colleagues suggest new ways of doing things, she *compares their ideas with other similar situations she has experienced* and uses this knowledge to evaluate the feasibility of the proposals.

Communication Style

People with the Stabiliser motivation pattern tend to talk about concrete, real-world things – the news, sport, the weather, family, work, facts and figures, who is doing what, and what is happening when. They often relate events in the present to their past experience.

They tend to speak in a factual and sequential way. If they are telling a story, they will start at the beginning and describe what happened in chronological order, concentrating on the facts and the sequence of events. They like others to do the same, and it often helps a Stabiliser if you tell them the topic you are going to talk about to give them a point of reference first, e.g. *"about the presentation tomorrow."*

Stabilisers tend to give detailed information and examples, and they value "common sense." They give an organised and controlled message. They may come across as formal and conventional – they usually plan their communication to be appropriate to the audience. They often ask questions beginning with "what" and "how" rather than "why," and they will ask for and give evidence.

They will often refer to things that happened in the past and may be surprised when others don't remember them. They like to share their experience and may ask others to share theirs. Sometimes they can frustrate their colleagues by appearing to get bogged down in detail.

THE THEORIST MOTIVATION PATTERN

Their Inner Drive

At the core of a Theorist's motivation pattern – why they do what they do – is the need to be **competent** and contribute to progress. They want to build and share their knowledge and expertise. They like to have intellectual independence.

The animal metaphor for this motivation pattern is the owl (Figure 3.5). Owls traditionally symbolise wisdom – the Greek goddess of wisdom, Athena, has an owl as her symbol. Owls can turn their heads almost to 360 degrees and so are able to take in a wide perspective. They have excellent night vision and can pinpoint their

Figure 3.5 The Theorist Motivation

prey and zoom in on them. These characteristics of owls represent the ability of Theorists to take in the big picture and to home in on the salient points or principles, to get to the core of the topic and the most important points.

Talents and Strengths

People with the Theorist motivation pattern are often described by others as:

Detached	Principled	Inventive	Sceptical
Analytical	Curious	Strategic	Logical
Ingenious	Creative	Competent	Objective
Autonomous	Precise	Organised	Resolute
Independent	Calm	Visionary	Confident
Theoretical	Preoccupied	Credible	Critical

They get their sense of purpose from their achievements, and they want to contribute to progress. They are independent thinkers and enjoy problem-solving. They like to design new and efficient ways of doing things, and they enjoy coming up with creative solutions to problems. Often these are systems and processes, rather than objects they might make with their hands, but they can include physical structures, ways of communicating, or anything that takes their interest.

They like models and theories and want to understand everything that interests them. They like to acquire knowledge and learn new things. They often bring creativity and innovative solutions and look for criteria and principles on which to make decisions. It is likely that Albert Einstein, Carl Jung, and Steve Jobs (co-founder of Apple) had the Theorist motivation pattern.

They tend to pay attention to associations and meanings and trust their insights and ideas about future possibilities. They tend to see the big picture first, before (possibly) going down into the details, and they see links with other aspects that are not always obvious to others. They don't take things on face value, and they "read between the lines" looking for what something *means*, rather than what it *is*.

Their unique talent is their strategic skills. They enjoy researching and brainstorming options and devising processes and long-range plans to implement them.

Theorists like to be recognised for their *ideas*.[6] They like debate and discussion and don't mind when other people disagree with them (unless it gets heated). Their favourite question is probably *"why?"*.

> *Dom* has the Theorist motivation pattern and runs a successful IT consulting business, doing systems design for clients who want to improve their business processes. He is regarded as an *expert* in this field, and he gets new and repeat business through recommendation. He enjoys his work – each new client is a *new challenge*, which requires *new solutions*, and he likes *researching, exploring, and evaluating options and coming up with new proposals* for them. He always *learns* something new on each project, and it makes him feel good when he sees his designs implemented. He also likes being an *independent* consultant – this gives him *control* over what he does and means he can always work on projects that interest him.
>
> *Sofia* is an architect, and she was asked to design a village as a blueprint for future civic planning. She loved working on this project. It enabled her to look at the *whole system* and draw in *ideas* from many different fields – climate change, green technologies, water usage, green modes of transport, energy efficiency, the future of work, how people spend their leisure time, and many more. She was able *to learn and expand her knowledge* and *apply her expertise* in architecture to design an exciting blueprint for the future.

Challenges

Often the things that we find challenging are the opposite of our strengths. People with the Theorist motivation pattern tend to focus on achieving the task rather than on creating a harmonious environment and:

- They may not consider the impact of their decisions on people
- They tend not to be so tuned in to other people's emotions or their own
- They don't always spot the need for sympathy
- They may forget to show appreciation or to praise effort rather than achievement
- They sometimes lose interest in the details of implementation

- They may avoid situations where there is a risk of feeling incompetent
- They tend to ask "why," which can cause others to react defensively

> *Carl* was a new team leader who needed to give feedback to a team member on a report she had done. He had a high need for *competence*, and he *hated to see mistakes* in anyone's work. He got *straight to the point* and told her what was wrong with the report. He was taken aback by her reaction – she was very upset and felt that the many hours of work she had put into it had not been appreciated. When we discussed this in a coaching session, he realised that he could have dealt with this differently by first praising her efforts, before indicating where changes were needed.

When making decisions, Theorists weigh up evidence and pros and cons impartially and often have a strong sense of fairness and justice. Even when they are personally involved in a situation, they can step outside of it and view it almost as an onlooker, applying their principles in an impartial way.

> At a workshop about decision-making, participants were given a scenario to discuss. The fictional business was in difficulty and needed to make one of its five sales people redundant. The participants were given information about their sales performance and personal lives and were asked to decide who to make redundant. The *Theorist* participants discussed and drew up a set of *criteria* that they applied *logically and impartially* to each sales person. They made their decision based on past sales performance and their predictions about important factors for the future. They did not give so much weight to personal circumstances (such as who most needed the income from the job).

Later you can compare how the Theorists behaved in this case study, with how the Catalysts behaved in the same situation.

What Theorists Need in a Job

People with the Theorist motivation pattern are often attracted to science, technology, and research (Figure 3.6).

Figure 3.6 Theorists at Work

They flourish in jobs where they can:

- Use their strategic skills to come up with innovative solutions to complex problems
- Work independently and have colleagues who also like to be independent
- Think for themselves and not stick to conventions if they don't see a reason for them
- Measure their achievements by their own high standards
- Receive recognition from people who they see as experts in their field
- Learn and increase their understanding of the topics of interest to them
- Work in an organisation that is involved in innovation, which could be in technical sciences, social sciences, or other fields
- Work in a role that involves research and design – e.g. engineering, marketing, IT, medicine, finance, university teaching

- Focus on possibilities for the future rather than on administering details in the present
- Use their ideas and imagination to create integrated systems that work better

More extraverted Theorists like to work with a variety of different people and often have good interaction and networking skills. More introverted Theorists tend to prefer working independently, at least initially until they are ready to share their ideas, or they choose to work with a small number of like-minded people who do not make too many demands on them.

> **Steve** is an **innovator**. He loves new technology and is always first in the office to try out new gadgets. He is **excited about new projects** and radiates his enthusiasm to the rest of the team. He has a long-term **vision** for implementing new ways of working in his department utilising the latest tools. He invites **experts** in to explore ideas with them, has **brainstorming** sessions, and maps out projects to implement the new tools, leaving more detailed planning to his team members.

Steve (above) is more extraverted, while Judi (below), who shares his Theorist drives for competence, expertise, and mastery, is more introverted and works in a different way.

> **Judi** is also an innovator. She was given the task of creating the content for a new look website for the charity she works for. She quietly set about **researching** other sites and, in parallel, thought through the purpose of the site, who it was for, what it should contain, and how it should look. Once she had established the initial **criteria**, she selected some specific users and had one-to-one meetings with them. This helped her refine her ideas, and she then put together a proposal for wider discussion.

Communication Style

People with the Theorist motivation tend to use abstract language. They enjoy talking about ideas and theories. These interest them more than the concrete world of people and things – the reality of who is doing what and what is happening when.

They enjoy speculating and asking "what-if" questions. They are often precise with language and choose just the right word to express their meaning. They are interested in connections between topics. They tend to be economical with their language, including relevant information, but without padding it out. Sometimes they don't state things that are obvious to them but may not be so obvious to others. They will often question what other people mean by the words they use, which can come across as nit-picking.

Their verbal and written communication can be lengthy. They often seek to impart their knowledge to enable others to have their depth of understanding, but this can be too detailed for others. They want to understand everything and assume others do too.

Sometimes their questioning can make them appear too critical. They can come across as arrogant when they believe they have more knowledge than others on a topic. They sometimes forget to show appreciation of other people's points of view, focusing on the task under discussion rather than on how people are reacting to them. They are more focused on getting to the *truth* in a debate rather than on maintaining *harmony* in the group.

THE CATALYST MOTIVATION PATTERN

Figure 3.7 The Catalyst Motivation

Their Inner Drive

At the core of a Catalyst's motivation pattern – why they do what they do – is a need to fulfil **potential** and be authentic. They want to make a difference for others. They like to have purpose or meaning that is connected to something beyond themselves.

The animal metaphor for this motivation pattern is the dolphin (Figure 3.7). Dolphins are sociable and playful animals. They have advanced forms of communication. They look after each other when one is injured, and they have also been known to help humans. Dolphins appear in Greek myths as a benevolent animal, a good omen for sailors. These characteristics of dolphins represent the Catalysts' desire to connect with others, to communicate and collaborate for the greater good, and to show empathy towards others.

Talents and Strengths

People with the Catalyst motivation pattern are often described by others using words such as:

Benevolent	Genuine	Romantic	Diplomatic
Enthusiastic	Collaborative	Innovative	Empathetic
Insightful	Optimistic	Creative	Sincere
Idealistic	Hyperbolic	Sensitive	Imaginative
Appreciative	Dramatic	Personable	Inspirational
Cooperative	Authentic	Credulous	Passionate

Harmony is very important to people with the Catalyst pattern, and they work hard to build bridges and find common ground between people. They often want to change the world to make it a better place for everyone. Nelson Mandela and Mohandas Gandhi probably had the Catalyst motivation pattern.

They are often imaginative and can bring creative solutions to problems, especially to activities that will help other people. They tend to focus more on the future than the past or present. They like to enable other people to develop and fulfil their potential, and they are motivated by creating possibilities and opportunities for people.

They tend to pay attention to associations and meanings and trust their insights and ideas about future possibilities. They tend to see the big picture first, before (possibly) going down into the details, and they see links with other aspects that are not always obvious to others. They don't take things on face value, and they "read between the lines," looking for what something *means*, rather than what it *is*.

Their unique talent is their diplomatic skills. They pick up nuances and anticipate the unspoken issues of other people and are empathetic. When people continue to disagree despite their best efforts, they can become very disheartened and may "take it personally." They like to live in a cooperative atmosphere, and they do not enjoy argument and competition.

Catalysts like to be recognised for *who* they are.[7] Their favourite question could be *"how can we all get along?"*.

> ***Stefan*** is a primary school teacher and has the Catalyst motivation pattern. He loves helping the children in his care to **grow and develop**. He likes to stimulate their **imagination** and open their minds to **connections** between different aspects of a topic, often with a focus on the **human impact**. Last year he arranged for a team of people from the Fairtrade organisation to visit the school, and he developed many different **themes and activities** from this for his class, which included crafts, care for the environment, how to grow food, and how people in other countries live. Stefan felt highly energised when he was planning this visit and the supporting lessons, as it tapped into his values of **respect for others**, **looking after the world**, and developing his pupils' understanding of the world and their **empathy for others**.
>
> ***Ronda*** is the marketing manager for a small business, which produces wooden flooring. At their weekly management meetings, there is often conflict between the production and engineering managers – each blaming the other for failures to meet production targets. Ronda **hates the critical atmosphere** and often acts as the **peacemaker**, pointing out that there was no point in blame but to focus instead on how to stop it happening again. She usually succeeds in **defusing the conflict**, and her colleagues respect her **diplomatic skills**. Sometimes she wishes that it didn't always fall on her to make peace.

Challenges

Often the things that we find challenging are the opposite of our strengths. Catalysts' focus on creating a harmonious environment can mean they avoid dealing with difficult issues and:

- They can be regarded by others as too idealistic and not sufficiently grounded in reality
- They may not weigh up the pros and cons of different decisions against objective criteria

- They sometimes avoid giving a critique of other people's points of view
- They may find it difficult to make tough decisions, which impact people
- Their ideas can be seen as impractical, which makes them feel hurt and unappreciated
- They are likely to take to heart any constructive feedback they receive and may take it more seriously than it was intended
- They sometimes lose interest in following through on the details or in maintaining routines

> *Daniela* had been working on a new project and felt she had put *a lot of herself* into the project. When she discussed progress on the project with her new manager, she was taken aback when he made some negative comments and seemed less than impressed with her work. Daniela's reaction was to *feel "offended" and "insignificant."* The impact of her manager's words was that it took several months before she felt able to continue work on the project.

When making decisions, Catalysts try to find an outcome that will promote harmony between people or is consistent with their values and beliefs. They want to take into account the human impact of any decision, and they put themselves into the other person's shoes and consider how they would feel in the situation.

> At a workshop about decision-making, participants were given a scenario to discuss. The fictional business was in difficulty and needed to make one of its five sales people redundant. The participants were given information about their sales performance and personal lives and were asked to decide who to make redundant. The *Catalyst* participants discussed the *personal circumstances* of each sales person and expressed their *sympathy* for them. They were *uncomfortable with having to make a decision that would have a big impact on somebody's life*. They eventually chose to make redundant the person whom they thought would be most able to find another job and survive financially. They did not give so much weight to past sales performance or predicted performance.

Compare how the Catalysts behaved in this case study, with how the Theorists behaved in the same situation (above).

What Catalysts Need in a Job

People with the Catalyst motivation pattern are often attracted to working with people (Figure 3.8).

They flourish in jobs where they can:

- Use their diplomatic skills to come up with creative solutions that will help people to grow
- Work in cooperation rather than competition and in a friendly, relaxed atmosphere without conflict or tension
- Work with other creative and caring people
- Receive regular positive feedback on their efforts – being appreciated for who they are, rather than what they have done
- Be led by someone who brings warmth and enthusiasm
- Have work that is consistent with their values and beliefs and where there is freedom to follow their inspiration

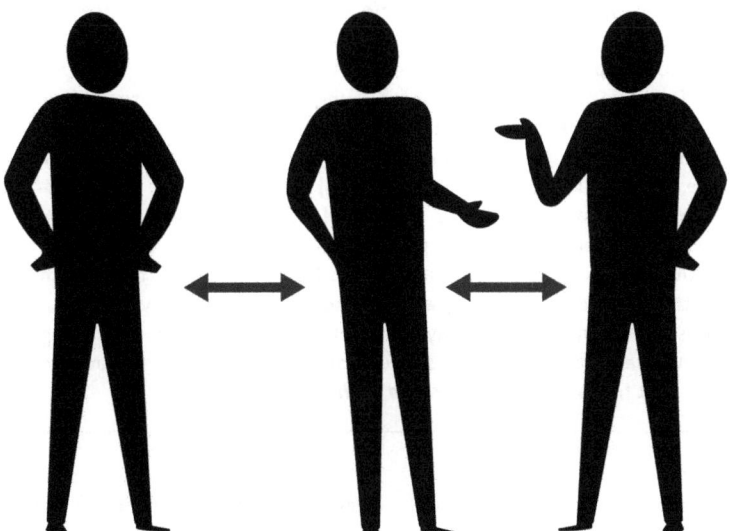

Figure 3.8 Catalysts at Work

- Work in a role that involves making a difference to other people or the world – e.g. training, teaching, counselling, and work in the creative industries
- Work in an organisation where they believe that the product or service has human value, such as in charities or religious work
- Use their ideas and imagination to change and improve the world around them

More extraverted Catalysts like to work with a variety of different people and are happy to be part of a team of supportive people whom they trust – they can feel inspired when working with others. More introverted Catalysts tend to prefer working alone uninterrupted, but they value the opportunity to bounce ideas around when they are ready. They also like working one-to-one where they can explore ideas or issues in depth.

> *Sanaa* loves her job. She works for a wildlife charity, and her role is to develop fundraising activities. She often comes up with ideas for ***new initiatives***, and she also involves colleagues in ***brainstorming*** sessions and ***networks with people*** from other charities. Once she has an idea, she is able to convert it into a ***creative message*** to attract people.
>
> *Danny* is a career counsellor for young people. His purpose in life is to help young people find their path, and he gets immense satisfaction from feeling he is ***helping them to grow and find out who they really are***. He loves his work and especially enjoys running large group sessions. In these sessions he is funny and entertaining, and he always succeeds in engaging young people. He introduces lots of ***different activities*** during the sessions and always has in mind how to run them so that ***everyone can enjoy participating***. He enjoys variety and never runs a session the same way twice. He gets young people thinking about ***their futures*** and what sort of work might suit them. He loves to feel that he has ***made a difference to their lives***.

Danny (above) is more extraverted, while Gina (below), who shares his Catalyst drives for making a difference and having a greater purpose, is more introverted and works in a different way.

> *Gina* is also a career counsellor and, like Danny, feels that she has found her purpose in life by *helping people become happier in their work*. She works with adults and always works one-to-one with them. This enables her to go into depth and explore with them their talents, values, and interests. She sometimes uses *creative techniques* such as collage to help them to surface their thoughts and feelings about their work and lives. Often people say afterwards that she has not only helped them to choose a career path but also helped them to *know themselves better* and to make *beneficial changes in their lives*.

Communication Style

Catalysts want to be in accord with others, and much of what they do and say is related to creating and maintaining harmony. Poor relationships with others are a big demotivator for Catalysts. They are naturally diplomatic and unlikely to be tactless with others.

They tend to use abstract language, and they talk about ideas and people, their beliefs and dreams. These interest them more than the concrete world of people and things – the reality of who is doing what and what is happening when. They like to talk about what might be in the future rather than what is practical now.

Catalysts tend to generalise when they talk and give general impressions rather than specific details. They tend to exaggerate and use more extreme language, such as "never," "always," "amazing," and "terrible." They may make leaps between topics, and other people may not see the connection between them.

Their verbal and written communication can sometimes be a little vague, giving lots of information but lacking clear requests or actions. They think they are being clear but use so many words and try so hard not to hurt other people's feelings that the other person may fail to get the message.

Sometimes they can appear too idealistic and fanciful to their more down-to-earth friends and colleagues. They sometimes avoid giving a critique of other people's points of view, being more concerned about how it might make someone feel, than on what is needed to get on with the task. They are more focused on maintaining *harmony* in the group than on getting to the *truth* in a debate.

SUMMARY

The four core motivators are linked to patterns of behaviour, and they influence what we are likely to want from a job, the strengths we bring to our work, the challenges we might face, and how we communicate. Knowing your own pattern of motivation and behaviour means you can both play to your strengths and develop yourself in other directions. Understanding these differences between people means that you can be more effective as a leader-manager, and adapt how you engage, develop, delegate, and connect, to motivate individual team members in different ways.

ACTION PLAN

Take a few moments to summarise your conclusions:

What have you learned about your own core motivator and behaviour pattern?

What is my top motivator?	
What are my strengths?	
How can I make the most of them?	
What are my challenges?	
How can I manage them?	
What really energises me in my work?	
How can I do more of that?	
How well does my communication work?	
What might I need to change?	

- What insights have you gained into the motivators and behaviour patterns of people in your team?
- Who might share your behaviour pattern? Who displays behaviours in line with other patterns?

Team Insights	
Improviser	
Stabiliser	
Theorist	
Catalyst	

Now that you know more about what motivates you and others, the next chapter looks at what you can do practically in relation to purpose – how you can Engage, Develop, Delegate, and Connect, to create a sense of common purpose for the team as well as tapping into individuals' own sense of purpose and core motivators.

NOTES

1. Grant, A. Professor of Management and Psychology at the Wharton School, Philadelphia, Twitter post, 30 January 2022.
2. These animal names were first used by David Keirsey.
3. Hodgson, D. (2012). *Personality in the Classroom*. Carmarthen: Crown House.
4. Csikszentmihalyi, M. (1990). *Flow: The Psychology of Optimal Experience*. New York: Harper Collins.
5. Hodgson, D. (2012). *Personality in the Classroom*. Carmarthen: Crown House.
6. Ibid.
7. Ibid.

LEADING ON PURPOSE

INTRODUCTION

By now I hope you are convinced that having a sense of purpose is essential for being motivated and for having well-being (Figure 4.1). You will have gained insight into the four core motivators and how these affect patterns of behaviour at work. You will also understand how your own top motivator might differ from what motivates your colleagues. We will look at what this means for your leadership style in Chapter 7.

This chapter is about what you can do practically in relation to purpose – how you can Engage, Develop, Delegate, and Connect, to create a sense of common purpose for the team as well as

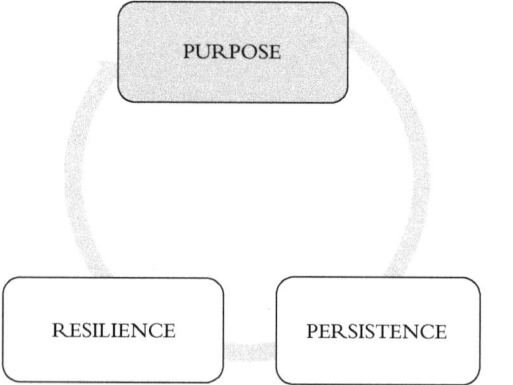

Figure 4.1 Motivation: Purpose, Persistence, and Resilience

DOI: 10.4324/9781003286646-5

tapping into individuals' own sense of purpose and core motivators (Figure 1.3).

> Happiness comes from using your signature strengths in the main realms of your life.[1] *Carroll Izard*

ENGAGE TO GIVE MEANING

The idea of "employee engagement" has been around for the whole of the 21st century. It was preceded in the last century by similar ideas often referred to as "employee participation" or "employee involvement" and various initiatives such as quality circles, suggestion schemes, and work councils.

Motivation and engagement are closely related – if an employee feels engaged, they will most likely be motivated to care about their team's goals and put in extra effort to achieve them. One view of engagement, proposed by Mayo,[2] is that it results from a combination of intrinsic and extrinsic motivation, plus a sense of personal well-being, and an absence of irritating factors. Every one of us can have a different personal mix of these elements, and it would be impossible for a leader-manager to satisfy all of them for everyone. However, you can become more aware of what is important to your team members and of your own personal mix.

The focus here is on how to engage your team in their work and in the organisation so that they can connect their work to a bigger goal and feel that what they do is meaningful. This is important to all of us, and particularly important to people with the Catalyst motivation pattern.

When people feel that their work has meaning, they feel an emotional connection with it – and with their team and the wider organisation. Having an emotional connection means they do things because they are committed to them, rather than merely compliant. They put in more effort and get better outcomes – and they feel happier.

Team Purpose

You may be part of several teams in your organisation (e.g. senior leadership team, project team, functional team, working group). You can relate the following activity to any of these teams.

What would you say is the purpose of your team? Why does your team exist?

My Team's Purpose

Try a thought experiment: How do you think other people see your team? What would your team members say was the purpose of the team? How do other parts of the organisation perceive your team? What would other colleagues in your organisation say?

What Others Might Say

If they all agree, then you are doing something right! But you may find that different groups have different opinions about what the purpose of your team is or should be. Even in a long-standing team, there will have been changes in the environment – in technology, customers, suppliers, the market – that have led to gradual changes in the roles and responsibilities of your team. In some cases, the original reason for the team to exist may have disappeared, and they may now be doing something completely different.

Sometimes there is a tendency to express a team's purpose in terms of targets in areas such as output, revenue, profit, growth, market share, cost reduction, sales, quality, and other operational key performance indicators. People are rarely inspired by these things. While they are important measures, it is better to express your team's purpose in terms of what it is your team **does** to reach those measurable targets.

People like to feel that their activities link to a wider purpose – this is more inspiring.

Here is an example of a purpose for an Accounts department in a company, expressed in two different ways:

1. Our purpose is to produce a set of accurate management accounts on time each month, quarter, and year
2. Our purpose is to provide financial forecasts and advice to the management team based on an accurate set of accounts,

produced on time each month, quarter, and year, so that they can make effective operational decisions

Here's another example for a Marketing department of a charity:

1. Our purpose is to upload content to the charity's website and social media accounts
2. Our purpose is to create engaging content for our website and social media accounts, which enhances the reputation of our charity and attracts people to become members or donate

And here is one for Maths teachers in a school:

1. Our purpose is to teach Maths to pupils in years 7–11 so they are well prepared for passing the end-of-year exams
2. Our purpose is to share our teaching strategies and approaches with each other so that we become more effective teachers and enable our pupils to enjoy Maths and be prepared for passing the end-of-year exams

In each case, which of the two statements inspires you more? Usually, people pick the second purpose as more inspiring. The second purpose is not only about the immediate output of the team; it is also about the impact of the work on others.

This is what motivates people – to know that their work means something beyond themselves, that it contributes to some bigger purpose or helps other people. Psychologically, it makes you feel significant, that you matter.[3]

Have a look back at the purpose you wrote earlier for your team. Does it show **why the work of your team is needed by others**? How would you amend it now?

Part of your role as a leader-manager is to help people find a sense of purpose at work by:

- Creating the "golden thread"[4] that enables them to see how their own job fits into the purpose of the team and how the team's purpose fits into the goals of the wider organisation
- Enabling them to draw on their own top motivator at work

By doing this, you create Meaning – you give people a sense of purpose.

You can motivate your team by working with them to articulate the team's purpose. This may be appropriate when there is a change in circumstances such as:

- The creation of a new team
- Downsizing of an existing team
- New people joining the team
- New projects
- Reorganisation
- Reinvigorating an existing team

The process of working together to agree the purpose results in more clarity about the task, greater commitment to it, and a positive climate in the team. As the leader-manager, you can set the scene with the broader context and set the boundaries for the discussion. Your voice will naturally carry more weight, and you may have to consciously hold back at times, to enable others to contribute.

Here is an outline of an activity to define your team's purpose. It works best with a facilitator from outside the team to run the process.

Defining Team Purpose

Set the context for the meeting, and invite your team to a session to clarify the team's purpose.

Begin by discussing with them:

- What is a team core purpose? (e.g. a statement of why we exist, our mission, our responsibilities)
- Who is it for? (e.g. the team or people outside the team?)
- What are the characteristics of an effective team purpose? (e.g. clear, memorable, free of jargon, inspiring, understandable by others, aligning to organisation's goals?)

Capture answers on a flip chart or virtual board.

Ask everyone to imagine and note down what their "elevator pitch" would be if they met the CEO in a lift and had 10 seconds to explain their team's purpose.

> Then split the team into three groups, and ask each of them to come up with a purpose for the team, and write it on a flip chart or virtual board.
>
> Ask each group to share their purpose, and explain what is important about it.
>
> Then, ask people to vote on which statement they think best reflects the team purpose, or choose keywords from each to create a new statement.
>
> Once you have agreed with your team's core purpose, discuss how you can all use it in your daily work, e.g.:
>
> - Put it on posters in the office
> - Include it in digital signatures
> - Include it as a header on meeting agendas
> - Use it to align roles and responsibilities in the team
> - Use it as a basis for setting objectives
>
> You may also want to identify measures of success; i.e. how would you know you were fulfilling your team's core purpose?

Relating the Team's Purpose to the Purpose of the Organisation

You can discuss with your team how their own activities fit into the wider aims of the whole organisation.

The Chartered Institute of Personnel and Development's (CIPD) research showed:

> That having a strong sense of organisational purpose that is shared by all employees, and often beyond, to include external stakeholders, is linked with engagement, satisfaction and sustainable business performance.

People usually feel happier at work if their sense of personal and team purpose aligns with the collective purpose of the organisation.

In the next case study, you can see the impact on motivation and performance of having a shared sense of purpose and processes in place that support people to be persistent and resilient.

You can also see the importance of attending to the three areas identified by John Adair's action-centred leadership model: achieving the task, building the team, and motivating individuals (see Chapter 1).

> *Phil*[5] became leader of a team of highly specialised design engineers in the aircraft industry. It first started as a "patchwork quilt" of individuals and activities characterised by high variety and low collective sense of direction and purpose. They faced a major challenge to improve their product performance and could no longer survive in disconnected silos. Phil recognised that to overcome the challenge they faced, the team needed to work more collaboratively, supporting each other more and sharing collective intelligence for broader impact. He recruited fresh people who were inspired by the opportunity, and together they created a shared vision and strategy to deliver these improvements.
>
> Looking back, he says there was a sense they were "a band of brothers," bringing product value fuelled by their collective passion and creativity and channelled by a common purpose. There was a clear link between their work on product performance and the company's strategic goal of increasing market share.
>
> The team introduced practical, simple governance and reporting to share successes and deal with or escalate contingencies. They held monthly technical briefings to do deep dives on specific topics. They reflected on experiences and made changes to the plan based on lessons learned in regular one-to-ones and team workshops. These contributed to greater team spirit, creating "a safe environment where we could openly share our ideas, hopes, fears and challenges ahead."

Individual Purpose

A natural follow-on from clarifying team purpose is to discuss individually with each team member:

1. Their own roles and responsibilities and how they fit into the team purpose
2. How well their role fits with their own sense of purpose

Here is a way to clarify roles and responsibilities:

> **Start/Stop/Continue Activity**
>
> Individual Roles and Responsibilities
> Use a flip chart and post-it notes or a virtual board.
> Ask your team member to list everything they do in a typical day, week, month – using one post-it per item.
> Then divide the post-its into activities that contribute towards fulfilling the purpose (either directly or indirectly via helping others in the team) and activities that are not related to the team purpose.
> Further subdivide these categories into activities that should **Stop** or **Continue**.
> Finally, what is missing? Is there anything that is not being covered? What might they need to **Start** doing in order to contribute to the team purpose?

Individuals are naturally motivated to do things that they enjoy and are good at. We often say that we do not have time for something, yet we do find time for other things. Tweaking team roles to enable people to make the most of their strengths and talents can encourage high performance. (Of course, you must be fair to all in doing this – not putting all the unpopular tasks on to one or two individuals.)

Some of your team members may have individual responsibilities that are not connected to the team purpose – e.g. special projects or activities they undertake for other parts of the organisation.

You can Use the Enjoy/Do Well matrix from Chapter 2 for individuals to review how well their role fits with their own top motivator. What would they put in each section?

	Enjoy	*Don't Enjoy*
Do well	*Talents – plan to do more?*	*Plan to reduce?*
Don't do well	*Potential strengths – plan to develop?*	*Plan to fix!*

Ask your team member to complete this template honestly, and then use it as the basis for discussion. It is likely that the things they are good at and do well relate to their core motivation. What is it about those things that particularly appeals to them?

- What do they really enjoy doing?
- How could their talents be better used in the team?
- What would they like to be better at?
- How could they reduce or fix the things they do not enjoy?
- What do they believe is their unique contribution to the team?
- What else would they like to do or be responsible for?

The conclusions they draw from this discussion will give them a greater sense of purpose in their work. They will have greater self-insight and will be better able to manage their own motivation.

It is possible that someone may feel that all their activities fall in the "Don't do well" boxes. This may need a more in-depth discussion, perhaps using a tool such as performance mapping (see next section) to explore further. You may also need to set expectations that it is unlikely that anyone would enjoy all aspects of their work 100% of the time and perhaps discuss what would be realistic – maybe above 60%?

The power of having a motivating purpose is shown in the story of Tess.

> ***Tess*** was a manager in a college of further education during the time of the COVID-19 pandemic, and she was given responsibility for implementing ways of delivering online learning solutions across all subject areas. She had to work on this from home – she missed face-to-face interaction with her colleagues and also had to cope with a busy household with her partner also working from home and with two school-age children and a dog at home too! But the difficult circumstances could not dampen her enthusiasm for this project. She was motivated and energised by the possibilities of this project to make learning for students even better than it had been before the pandemic, and this vision gave her the drive and determination to make it succeed. She told me that "some good things will come out of the pandemic lockdown – I know we can improve the education and the life chances of our students." She had a purpose that motivated her, and this drove her determination to persist.

What else could you do to Engage your team to give Meaning?

Engaging My Team

DEVELOP TO BUILD COMPETENCE

Feeling competent is one of the core motivators for all of us. People like to feel that they are using their talents, are good at their jobs, and are seen as competent by others. This is particularly important to people with the Theorist motivation pattern.

As a leader-manager, you are expected to ensure your team members are well matched to their roles and have the knowledge, skills, and attitudes to perform them effectively. Your organisation will have its own templates and processes for giving feedback, appraising performance, developing capability, and dealing with poor performance.

This section is about how to use the desire for competence as a motivating tool with your team members. Too often appraisal processes focus on weaknesses and how to overcome them. In practice, in most cases, you get better performance when you focus on strengths. Strengths are motivating; weaknesses are not.

The Learning Cycle

Adults learn and become more competent from doing things, from experience – but only if they take the time to review the experience and draw conclusions from it (Figure 4.2).

Your role as a manager is to create the space for your team members to review their experience. While appraisals are usually a summary of performance over a long period of time, a conversation based on the Learning Cycle[6] can be used for one-off events, e.g. after a meeting, presentation, phone call, and interaction with a colleague.

You can also use this model with the whole team, e.g. to review what went well or not during a meeting or to conduct a "lessons learned" activity at the end of a project.

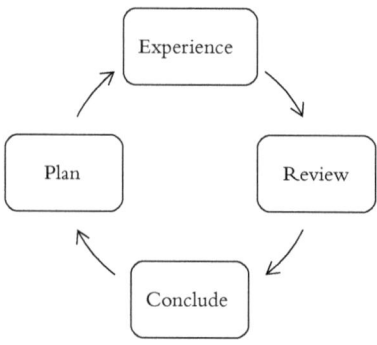

Figure 4.2 Kolb's Learning Cycle

Here is the process for using this framework with a team:

1. Ask them what they think went well
2. Ask them what they think didn't go so well
3. Ask them what they have learned from this and what conclusions they have drawn
4. Ask them, with the benefit of hindsight, what they would do differently in a similar situation next time

What Went Well?	*What Didn't Go So Well?*
What Did You Learn?	*What Would You Do Differently Next Time?*

Reviewing what has gone well is powerful, because it can enable your team or individuals to work out what exactly they did that made the event go well. This helps them to recognise their own talents – which they may take for granted - and this builds their confidence, which in turn boosts their performance.

The Enjoy/Do Well matrix in the last section can be used as a way into a conversation about developing capability – for example, which talents are under-utilised, which potential strengths can be further developed, which "don't enjoy/don't do well" areas can be minimised.

Performance Mapping

Another useful way to help individuals develop their competence is to analyse with them any difficulties they have in their performance, to find the root cause of the problem. People are often semi-aware that something is not working well for them but do not stop to work out the underlying issue or how to deal with it. Your role as a leader-manager is to help them identify the source of any problem and come up with a plan for resolving it.

The diagram shows the main factors within a person – related to competence – that influence how well they perform at work (Figure 4.3). (There are others, external to the person, that also influence their performance – such as technology, resources, processes, team-working, and opportunity – but here I want to focus on the individual factors.)

You can think of personal competence in any situation as a combination of:

- What knowledge is required to do this?
- What skills are needed?
- What behaviours will be effective in this situation?
- How motivated is the person to get it done?

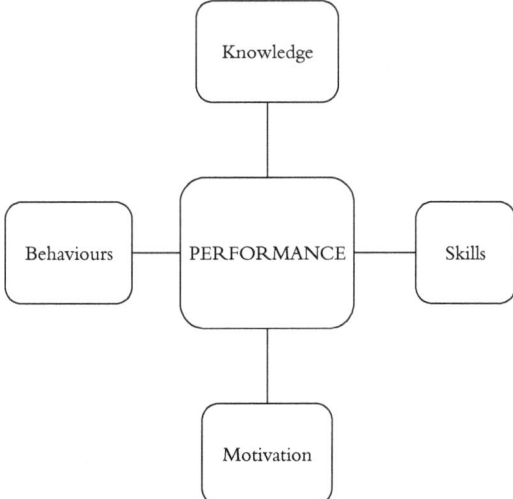

Figure 4.3 Performance Mapping

In the case study below, the potential source of the problem could have been any of these four areas.

> *Sam* works for an IT company. Part of her role is to market products and services to agencies that, if they are convinced, promote them to their clients. Sam has noticed that when she attends meetings with the agencies, along with a colleague, the agency representatives always look to her colleague for confirmation of Sam's proposals. Sam feels undermined and is beginning to lose confidence in her ability. She is about to launch a new product to the agencies and is worried that she may not be able to convince them to sell it. She decides to discuss this with her manager.
>
> Her manager, *Jess*, is surprised to hear that Sam is worried – she has great respect for Sam's technical competence and for her work ethic. Jess conducts a coaching conversation to explore the problem with her. Jess has the four areas of knowledge, skill, behaviour, and motivation in the back of her mind. They conclude that:
>
> *Knowledge*: Sam has good knowledge of the product, how it would fit into the agencies' portfolios, and what the key decision-makers would want.
>
> *Skills*: Sam has the technical skills to demonstrate the benefits of the product and can produce an engaging presentation with convincing data.
>
> *Behaviour*: Sam has a quiet manner and is not particularly assertive – when she is asked questions, she likes to think first before answering. She can come across as indecisive.
>
> *Motivation*: Sam is feeling unsure about herself in this role and starting to wonder if she is in the right job, and this is undermining her confidence and ability to have an impact.
>
> Jess and Sam concluded that the likely source of the problem was Sam's behaviour. They agreed several actions to help Sam become more assertive and project a more confident manner. She left the meeting feeling relieved to have aired her worries, buoyed up by Jess's support for her, and happy that she could see a way forward.

Once you identify the root cause of the problem, then you can work with your team member to come up with relevant potential solutions.

Performance mapping can be applied to the whole team; e.g. you can map the mix of knowledge, skills, and behaviours in the team to determine where there might be gaps or where there are unused talents.

Other ways to build individual competence, such as by giving feedback and coaching, are covered in the next chapter.

What else can you do to enable team members to develop their competence? How could you use your regular meetings (e.g. one-to-ones) in a different way?

Building Competence

Recognising Demotivation

The case study above illustrates the feedback loops between performance, behaviour, and motivation. As a leader-manager, you should be alert to what is going on in your team and ready to pick up on any signs that something is not quite right. We often avoid dealing with tricky situations, hoping that they will go away. But they are more likely to worsen if not picked up. Here are some signals to watch out for:

- Changes in performance
- Changes in behaviour
- Not getting tasks done on time
- Being easily distracted
- Being late or absent
- Doing personal tasks at work
- Not responding to requests from others
- Not engaging with the rest of the team – or too much engagement!
- Downbeat body language

The most effective way to deal with this is to have an open conversation with the person to share what you have noticed and ask for their comments. Then you can work with them to come up with appropriate solutions. See Chapter 7 for guidance on having difficult conversations.

DELEGATE TO GIVE FREEDOM

The desire to have some choice and control over what we do is one of the four core motivators and is particularly important to individuals with the Improviser motivation pattern.

How can you give people in your team more choice and control over what they do, how they do it, and perhaps also over when and where they do it? Setting and agreeing goals is one way and we will look at this in the next chapter. Being clear on roles and responsibilities, as discussed above, is another way. This section looks at what stops us delegating and what and how to delegate.

Barriers to Delegating

We are sometimes reluctant to delegate. It can be difficult to balance the need to delegate with the desire to retain control, and it can seem easier just to do more yourself. But in the long run, this is not sustainable – you get burnt out and your team members do not feel trusted. Not delegating can also prevent your own development.

When we get promoted, we tend to do more of what made us successful at the lower level. However, what is needed at a higher level is always different from what enabled you to succeed at the level below. Therefore, doing more of the same is not the answer, and you have to learn to use your team in a different way – and part of this is how and what you delegate.

What stops you delegating?

Barriers to Delegating

We often think we don't have time to delegate, or that it's quicker to do something ourselves, or that we don't want to "dump" things on our teams. But the benefits of delegation are:

- It gives individuals an opportunity to develop their capability
- It provides flexibility during absence
- They feel trusted and more significant

- They take responsibility
- They get exposure to other parts of the organisation
- It enables workload to be shared more equitably

How could you reframe how you think about delegation?

Reframing Delegation	
How can I overcome the barriers?	
How could delegating help me and others?	

What to Delegate

Extra tasks often come up at work, in addition to agreed roles and responsibilities, and you decide to whom to delegate them. Sometimes you might automatically delegate them to the person you know will do it fastest or who has done it before. But it is worth considering other factors such as:

- Who might benefit from doing it?
- Who needs the experience?
- Who has the time to do it?
- What could they bring to the task?

It's also worth thinking about why you are delegating and what's in it for them. If you ask somebody at short notice to attend an important meeting in your place, this is not delegation – this is to help you, so you should make it clear that you are asking for help. However, if you ask someone to attend an important meeting in your place to give them the exposure to more senior colleagues, this is part of their development – provided you review the experience with them afterwards so they learn from it.

As well as delegating tasks, you may be able to give your team members some choice over when and how they perform their roles. Now that working from home is becoming more widespread, there is an expectation of flexibility. Using the opportunity of flexible working wisely can enhance motivation in your team.

How to Delegate

Most people are motivated when they feel they have some autonomy over what they do and how they do it, so it is important to delegate in such a way as to maximise their sense of empowerment. It's also important to provide support when you delegate so as not to overwhelm people with too much responsibility before they are ready.

Here are some tips for delegating in a way that achieves "supported empowerment":

- Decide on **areas of responsibility** to delegate rather than one-off tasks
- Clarify your **expectations** with the person to whom you are delegating
- Delegate the responsibility with the appropriate **authority** to carry out the task
- Ask open questions to ensure they **understand and agree**, e.g. *"what are your thoughts?", "how will this affect you?", "how will you go about it?", "when can we review progress?"*
- Agree with the person how you are going to **monitor** it and what progress reporting is required
- Monitor progress on the due dates as agreed, not before
- Ensure the person agrees to do it and has the **skills** to do it, and find out what help they might need from you or others
- Use delegation to give people the **opportunity to learn and develop**, not just to dump tasks on them that you don't want to do

How else can you give some choice and control to your team over their work?

Giving Freedom

CONNECT TO CREATE BELONGING

We are social beings. For most of us, our relationships – especially our relationships with friends and family outside work – are the most important part of our lives. Having good relationships with people at work is important too.

Feeling that you belong to a team, a group, or an organisation is a fundamental part of our social existence and is one of the core motivators. It is particularly important to those with a Stabiliser motivation pattern. I refer to it as "belonging"; other psychologists refer to it as relatedness,[7] or affiliation,[8] or inclusion.[9] Part of your role as a manager is to create this sense of connection to each other in the team so people feel they belong to the group and want to work towards its common purpose.

With the growth of hybrid working, this is becoming more difficult. The social ties between people at work may weaken when they do not meet in person so often or share common experiences. This can lead to them becoming less committed to the organisation.

How you communicate has an impact on how connected people feel to their colleagues and the organisation. Here are some factors to consider:

1. The impact of your own communication on others
2. How to create psychological safety within your team
3. Building trust

(Chapter 7 covers how to address any unhelpful behaviour in your team and how to deal with conflict.)

Intention, Impact, and Influence

As a manager you automatically have people's attention. To have their respect, you need to be able to communicate well. To do this you need to know the people you are managing and how to adapt your own style to suit where appropriate.

When we communicate with other people, we usually have a positive intention, but sometimes the way we come across can have a negative impact, and then we don't have the influence we want (Figure 4.4). Being aware of your own behaviour and whether your impact matches what you intended is an essential basis for creating connection in your team. Because you are the manager, people see you as a role model; they will observe how you behave, what you do, and what you say. You set the tone for the team.

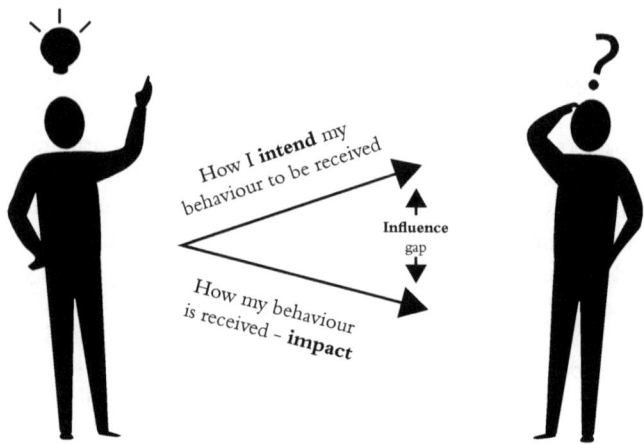

Figure 4.4 Intention, Impact, and Influence

We judge other people by their impact on us (e.g. *"he was rude!"*), but we judge ourselves by our intention (*"I didn't mean to be rude, I just wanted to…"*). Really it should be the other way around – we should make allowances for other people, give them the benefit of the doubt, and judge ourselves by our impact.

For example:

- You might have the positive intention of getting quick achievable results but come across as impatient and demanding
- You might want to ensure there is a carefully thought-through plan before acting, but your team might see you as slow and inflexible
- You may be trying to weigh up lots of information to get the best possible result but your team may see you as indecisive and unassertive
- You may be attempting to generate enthusiasm but might come across as flustered and frantic

When you are under pressure, how do you behave? What are your worst habits? What impact could this have on the people around you?

My Intention ... and My Impact

Learning how to adapt your style and being more emotionally intelligent is covered further in Chapter 7 and in my book, *How to Get On with Anyone*.[10]

Creating Psychological Safety

Research within Google[11] found five factors that set apart high-performing teams. The top predictor of high performance was a sense of psychological safety, which comes from how the team members interact with each other.

> No one person has all the answers ... your job as a leader is to capture the collective intelligence of your team.[12]

You can only capture the collective intelligence of your team if they feel able to speak up, to make suggestions, to risk mistakes. Have you ever been in a meeting when no one is willing to say anything? Or people wait until the boss has spoken first? This does not lead to the best outcomes. We are increasingly realising the benefits of diversity of thinking and approaches,[13] and if you want to get the best results, then encouraging psychological safety – an atmosphere where people will speak up and be vulnerable in front of each other – is essential.

One way to encourage a climate where people speak up is based on the support and challenge model.[14] Check what behaviours you demonstrate yourself and encourage in your team. Teams need to show both supportive and challenging behaviours to achieve high performance (in this context, "challenging behaviour" does not mean difficult or inappropriate, but it means being prepared to question or express different opinions – this helps avoid groupthink[15]).

As you can see from Figure 4.5, the best position is the top right-hand box, with high support and high challenge. This combination can lead to an energised team, while support without challenge, or challenge without support, can lead to an ineffective climate, either too cosy or too stressful.

Supportive behaviours could include:

- Giving praise
- Offering to help

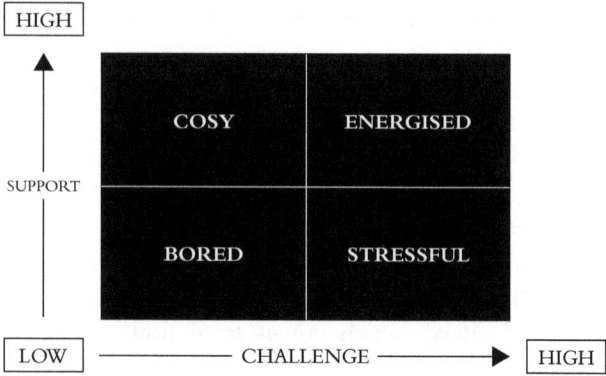

Figure 4.5 Support and Challenge Matrix

- Showing empathy
- Making time to talk
- Promoting their ideas
- Listening to their concerns

Challenging behaviours could include:

- Asking "why" questions
- Proposing alternatives
- Pointing out problems
- Stating difficulties
- Disagreeing

Sometimes people may deliberately play "devil's advocate" – this is ok, as long as they tell their colleagues that this is what they are doing.

What could you do to encourage both support and constructive challenge in your team?

Encouraging Support and Challenge

Creating an inclusive culture may also mean discouraging excessive "banter" in the team, as this can lead to some individuals being excluded from the in-group and not able to make their contribution. See Chapter 7 for guidance on dealing with unhelpful behaviours.

Building Trust

I often ask people whom in the management team they trust most. They usually say their immediate manager more than people at higher levels. Getting to know people on a personal level develops trust. This is more difficult online, so finding virtual alternatives to the coffee machine chat is important – and making time to talk about personal things, not just the tasks.

Much of our communication at work is at the level of rituals, facts, and perhaps ideas.[16] We tend to be more cautious about sharing our opinions and judgements, and it's even more rare that we share our feelings. As people move from talking about facts and ideas to revealing more about their own feelings and values, the level of risk increases, but so does the level of trust and commitment. Taking the risk of revealing more about your own feelings, values, and beliefs will engender trust in your team. It also gives permission to your team members to raise worries or concerns with you, and it's an opportunity for you to build a supportive relationship with them.

Trust is earned by how you deal with people, what you do and say, and how far your words match your deeds. Managing others puts you in a position of power, and it means you have a responsibility to use your influence ethically. Being authentic and willing to show your vulnerability builds trust and encourages others to do the same, creating a climate of psychological safety in your team.

What else can you do to connect to create belonging in your team?

Creating Belonging

TIPS FOR THE TOP MOTIVATORS

When engaging, developing, delegating to, and connecting with individuals, you may be able to adapt your approach to fit with their personal top motivators. If you are not sure what they are, you can try out different approaches. If there is a person in the team with whom you have difficulty, assume their motivation pattern is the one that least resonates with you (check back to Chapter 2). The table below gives some tips for flexing.

	Improviser	Stabiliser	Theorist	Catalyst
Core need	Freedom To have some choice and control in how they do their job	Belonging To belong to the group and feel valued for contributing to it	Competence To use their talents and feel they are good at their job	Potential To be true to themselves and help others be the best they can be
Motivated when they can…	Be noticed Make an immediate concrete impact Have freedom to act Get impressive quick results	Be responsible. Contribute to the group Have structure and consistency Respect tradition and continuity	Be competent Bring knowledge and expertise Have intellectual independence Contribute to progress	Be authentic Make a difference to others and the world Have purpose or meaning Fulfil potential
Engage to give meaning: Show how the team purpose will let them…	Focus on the pragmatic here and now – in a spontaneous way Be impressive Give them the opportunity to have fun	Focus on the pragmatic here and now – in a structured way Do their duty Give them a framework to work within	Focus on the future and on tasks Show mastery Give them the opportunity to learn	Focus on the future and on people Use their unique skills Make things better for others

LEADING ON PURPOSE

	Improviser	*Stabiliser*	*Theorist*	*Catalyst*
Develop to build competence: Offer them learning which…	Is hands-on and they can try out Is useful and practical Is challenging and fun Has variety and movement Shows what's in it for them	Has precise, step-by-step instructions They can repeat and practise Enables steady progress Has practical outcomes Is useful	Includes independent work Allows them to research for themselves Is underpinned by sound theory Includes concepts and ideas Is taught by experts	Fosters personal growth Involves others Includes ideas about people Gives them frequent positive feedback Is led by someone warm and enthusiastic
Delegate to give freedom: Give them tasks which enable them to…	Solve problems in the moment and see immediate results	Work with others to get practical results	Learn new things and work with experts	Help others develop and grow
Connect to create belonging: Build rapport with them by using their style…	*Their style is:* *Spontaneous* *Casual* Be brief and specific Focus on the present and the facts Use humour	*Their style is:* *Factual* *Traditional* Be specific with facts and details Explain next steps and actions Give evidence	*Their style is:* *Rational* *Pros and cons* Give the overall picture Let them question and give input. Explain the logic and benefits	*Their style is:* *Warm* *Harmonious* Connect with them personally Give the overall picture Show the benefits for people

SUMMARY

This chapter has been about "what" motivates us. We have seen how to **Lead on Purpose** – by clarifying your team's purpose and using specific tools and techniques to engage, develop, delegate to, and connect with your team to appeal to the four core motivators that we all share.

In the next chapter, we will look at "how" we are motivated – the processes that enable us to sustain our motivation over time – and how the leader-manager can facilitate that in their teams.

ACTION PLAN

Capture your ideas about specific actions you could take in these four management capability areas.

Engage	Develop	Delegate	Connect

NOTES

1 Izard, C. E. (1993). "Four Systems for Emotion Activation: Cognitive and Non-cognitive Processes." *Psychological Review*, Vol. 100, No. 1, 68–90.
2 Mayo, A. (2019). "The Individualism of Motivation." *Strategic HR Review*. https://doi.org/10.1108/SHR-03-2019-0016.
3 Schutz, W. (1958). *FIRO: A Three Dimensional Theory of Interpersonal Behaviour*. New York: Rinehart.
4 Chartered Institute of Personnel and Development. (2010). "Shared Purpose: the Golden Thread?"
5 Phil Bradshaw, Talent & Executive Management Coordinator UK, Airbus.
6 Kolb, D.A. (1984). *Experiential Learning: Experience as the Source of Learning and Development*. Englewood Cliffs: Prentice Hall.
7 Alderfer, C. P. (1972). *Existence, Relatedness, and Growth: Human Needs in Organizational Settings*. New York: Free Press.
8 McLelland, D. (1961). *The Achieving Society*. Princeton: Van Nostrand.
9 Schutz, W. (1958). *FIRO: A Three Dimensional Theory of Interpersonal Behaviour*. New York: Rinehart.
10 Stothart, C. (2018). *How to Get On with Anyone*. Harlow: Pearson.
11 Google 2012, "Project Aristotle." See Amy Edmondson of Harvard.
12 Heffernan, M. (2015) *Beyond Measure: The Big Impact of Small Changes*, Simon & Schuster, New York.

13 Syed, M. (2021). *Rebel Ideas*. London: John Murray.
14 I cannot find the original source for this well-known model. I first came across it in 1992 when facilitating groups of leaders in self-development.
15 Janis, I. L. (1982). *Groupthink: Psychological Studies of Policy Decisions and Fiascoes*. Boston, MA: Houghton Mifflin.
16 Powell, J. (1999). *Why Am I Afraid to Tell You Who I Am?* Michigan: Zondervan.

PERSISTENCE AND PERFORMANCE

INTRODUCTION

If you work in a job and in an organisation where you:

- Have a sense of purpose
- Have some freedom to act
- Can hone your competence
- Feel that you belong
- Have the opportunity to fulfil your potential

then you most likely feel pretty happy. But even when you work in a role like this, there will still be some occasions when you feel demotivated and some aspects of your job that you do not enjoy.

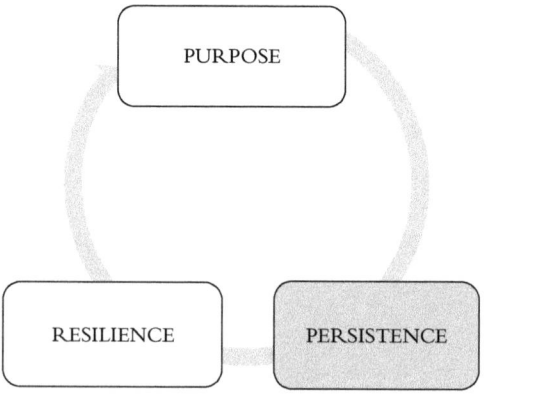

Figure 5.1 Motivation: Purpose, Persistence, and Resilience

DOI: 10.4324/9781003286646-6

In practice, it would be unrealistic to think that you could spend 100% of your time on things that excite and energise you. Every job has aspects we are not so keen on (see your Enjoy/Do Well matrix!). There are times when we need some help to sustain our motivation.

> Performance equals potential minus interference.[1] *Timothy Gallwey*

The first part of this chapter covers the psychology behind persistence (Figure 5.1) and encourages you to try out some of the practices for yourself.

The second part is about three core management practices, which, if you get right, can have a big impact on your team members' motivation. These are:

- Setting motivating goals
- Giving feedback that works
- Coaching to build confidence in ability, i.e. self-belief

There is also guidance on managing virtual and global teams and on creating a culture of persistence in your team.

WHAT IS PERSISTENCE?

Persistence is about **how** we keep ourselves motivated. The dictionary definition of persistence is to *continue firmly or obstinately in an opinion or a course of action in spite of difficulty or opposition.*[2] Difficulties often come from our own thoughts and self-limiting beliefs. I see persistence as:

> Managing thoughts, beliefs and emotions to stay positive and confident.

How we think and feel has an enormous impact on our motivation. As a leader-manager, you influence – whether you intend to or not – what people think and feel by what **you** do and say. **Your** behaviour influences **their** thoughts and emotions, so it is important to be intentional about what you do and what you say.

Think about your current or a previous manager. What do they do or say that makes you feel positive? What do they do or say that can make you feel less positive?

Behaviours	Impact

Thoughts and Self-belief

Kelly Holmes[3] (former British middle-distance athlete and winner of double gold medals at the 2004 Olympics) believes self-belief comes from

> Finding something in life that makes you feel good about yourself.

For her, the key ingredients include:

- Recognising what you are good at – being aware of your talent
- Seeing others succeed and realising you can do it too
- Attributing your success to things you can control (e.g. to practice or technique)
- Learning from failures – having a growth mindset
- Building forward one step at a time

You can see from her list that how she thinks about her performance is important for maintaining her self-belief.

One of the first books I read about coaching was Timothy Gallwey's *The Inner Game of Work*, which drew on his experience in sports, especially tennis and golf. Gallwey suggested that

> Performance = potential minus interference

– with the interference coming from our own thoughts and emotions. He wrote that

> The opponent within one's own head is more formidable than the one on the other side of the net.

Sometimes our performance in a situation does not match our potential, because of interference caused by our own unhelpful thoughts. If you let FUD creep in – fear, uncertainty, and doubt – this undermines your confidence and your performance. Here is an example of the thoughts someone had before going for a job interview and how they replaced them with more helpful thoughts:

Unhelpful Thoughts	*Replace with Helpful Thoughts*
There's a lot of competition	I've got as much chance as anyone
I haven't got the skills for this role	I've got skills in xyz
They already know who they want	They want the best person and that could be me
I'm no good at interviews	I've prepared well

The thoughts on the left-hand side undermined their confidence and would have affected how they behaved at the interview – they would look and sound less confident. By focusing on the thoughts on the right-hand side, they felt more confident, and this was reflected in their body language and voice – they stood taller, made more eye contact, and spoke more assertively. Saying the things on the right-hand side to themselves is "positive self-talk" – telling yourself things that will help you, rather than hinder you, in the situation.

What often works is to think about the *process* (i.e. what you can control) rather than the *outcome* (what you can't control). An elite sportsperson cannot control the **outcome** of a race – other athletes might perform better than them on the day. However, they can control the **process** of preparing for and running the race to give themselves the best chance of winning. Similarly, the person going for the job interview can't guarantee they will get the job, but they can give themselves the best chance by how they think and feel about it.

Try this for yourself. Think of a current task or a project that you feel unsure about. Note down your unhelpful thoughts. Are your thoughts logical and realistic? What would an outsider say about them? How could you turn them into a more helpful perspective?

Unhelpful Thoughts	Replace with Helpful Thoughts

Competence and Confidence

The helpful thoughts must be grounded in reality – there is no point in telling yourself that you can achieve something that is clearly unrealistic. Competence and confidence are not always related. This is particularly apparent in selection interviewing. Some people are skilled at "impression management,"[4] and their confidence can lead the interviewer to assume they are competent.

More often it works the other way around. One of my interviewees[5] for this book commented that often people are competent but do not have enough confidence in their own ability, which means that they do not display their talents and skills – a loss both for them personally and for their organisation.

How we talk to ourselves about our successes and failures – and what we hear other people saying about us – is important for maintaining persistence. **If we attribute success or failure to things we can control, this leads to more helpful thoughts**, rather than attributing it to luck or other random factors.[6]

We know that people perform better when they feel more confident. This is one reason why football teams usually play better at home than away – the support of the home crowd makes them feel confident, and they perform better. Talk to any sportsperson, and they will tell you that it is important for their performance to manage how they think and feel – it is as important as their physical and technical capability. This is tennis player Novak Djokovic, speaking after winning the French Open in 2021, about how he came back after losing the first two sets:

> I told myself I can do it, encouraged myself, I strongly started to repeat that inside of my mind, tried to live it with my entire being.

His opponent, Tsitsipas, did not give up and carried on fighting until the end. Though disappointed, he knew he had done everything he could:

> I am happy with the way I performed, the way I tried things, even if they didn't work.

This is a much more helpful thought for his future performance rather than feeling downhearted because he was beaten.

Managing your thoughts and feelings and doing some positive self-talk, so that you feel confident, are essential for you – or your team members – to persist and be motivated.

And it means that one of the most powerful things you can do for your team members is to be *intentional* in what you do and say so that you build their confidence in their capability and thereby enable them to persist.

We will see how to do this later in this chapter.

Beliefs and Emotions

What we think and believe about ourselves, other people, and the situation has a big impact on how we feel about it and hence on the results we get. Our beliefs can act:

- As accelerators and help us feel positive and achieve what we want or
- They can act as brakes and hinder us from feeling motivated and achieving what we want

Managing your thoughts and beliefs – so they help rather than hinder you – is a key part of sustaining your motivation.

Our beliefs and thoughts influence how we feel, so we need to be aware of our emotions if we are to persist. Human beings are not only rational beings but emotional ones too. Emotions have a big impact on our motivation to act – in fact "emotion" and "motivation" have the same Latin root meaning, "to move." It is often how we **feel** about something that makes us act rather than how we **think** about it. This is why charities appeal to

108 PERSISTENCE AND PERFORMANCE

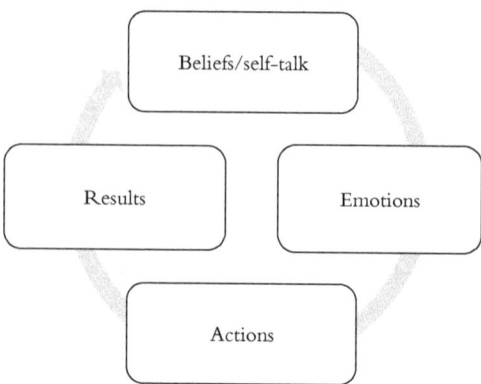

Figure 5.2 The BEAR chain

our emotions rather than our rational thinking when they want us to donate to their cause.

Neuroscientists believe that how we think and feel are "completely intertwined."[7] There is a chain reaction from our thoughts and beliefs to our feelings and actions and to the results we get, which I call the BEAR Chain (Figure 5.2).

This chain can work positively or negatively.

Think of a recent situation when you have experienced this chain reaction, either positively or negatively. What were your beliefs about the situation/yourself/the others? What were your feelings? What did you say and do? And what impact did your actions have on the result?

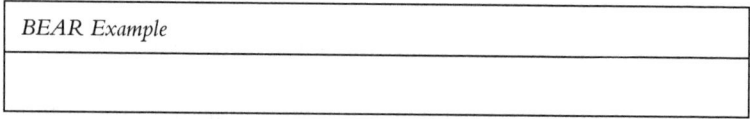

We've looked at the psychology behind persistence and the importance of having helpful thoughts, beliefs, and feelings if we are to persist. Now let's go on to what you can do as a leader-manager to help your colleagues reduce their interference, build confidence in their ability, and sustain their motivation.

Remember that what *you* do and say influences how *they* think and feel. And how they think and feel impacts their motivation and performance.

THE LEADER-MANAGER'S ROLE

To stay motivated – to persist – people need to know:

- What they are expected to achieve
- How they are doing
- How to solve problems

The next sections cover three management practices that address these needs:

- Setting motivating goals
- Giving feedback that works
- Coaching to build confidence in ability – self-belief

Your organisation will most likely have formal processes for goal setting, reviewing performance, and developing skills. This book is not about those formal processes – it is about how you can connect with your team members to motivate them. Sometimes the formal processes become an end in themselves, and the positive intentions behind them are lost. Some organisations link them to pay for performance, which is an unhelpful distraction when you want to create an honest and motivating discussion.

You may not be able to change the formal processes in your organisation, but you can change the **quality of the conversations you have with your team members** – what you say and do – both within and outside the formal processes. The guidelines that follow are about HOW to set goals, give feedback, and coach in a way that gives you maximum chance of creating a motivating environment.

SETTING MOTIVATING GOALS

Goal setting theory[8] is one of the academic theories about motivation that has filtered into society and is commonly used in organisations of all types, as well as in people's personal lives.

Setting goals is an enabler to achieving what we want. Goals are not only about the end result; they are also about the path to follow to get there. Within the overall purpose of the team, or the individuals' sense of their own purpose, there are a range of smaller goals and tasks to be achieved. These may be a mixture of "process" goals and "outcome" goals. Having goals, and a realistic plan to achieve them, enables you to persist.

Principles for Setting goals

Set SMARTER Goals

Many people are familiar with the idea that goals should be SMART – specific, measurable, achievable, realistic, and time-bound. Some organisations add extra elements such as "exciting and rewarded."

Let Your Team Participate in Setting Goals

Research has shown that when people participate in setting their own goals, they are more likely to accept them and be committed to them. When people are committed, rather than merely compliant, they will put in more effort.

Apply the Goldilocks Principle

The tasks you set for yourself (or others) need to be "just right" – not too easy, nor too difficult. If they are too easy, you will get bored, and if too difficult, you will be discouraged and give up. To be motivating, they need to have the right amount of stretch so that you will feel a sense of achievement when you reach them.

Break an Elephant Task into Mouse-Sized Bites

A big task or project can seem daunting, and it can be hard to get started. Breaking it down into a series of smaller goals, tasks, or steps makes it easier to make progress. You can then develop a plan of action to achieve each element.

Reward Effort As Well As Achievement

Sometimes people can put in a lot of effort but not reach the desired results due to factors outside their control; other times they can get good results without a lot of effort. It can be demotivating for team members if you do not recognise their effort.

Plan for the Planning Fallacy

Human beings have a blind spot about what can realistically be achieved. We consistently underestimate how long it will take to carry out a task – this is why major construction projects frequently come in late and over budget. When you are setting timescales, assume that things will go wrong and that unexpected things will happen – plan extra time for this.

Focus on A

The "A" in SMARTER usually refers to achievable or attainable. It's the most important letter and the one that we spend almost no time on. To make a goal attainable, we need to plan how to get there in detail. It's at this stage that you sometimes discover that there are dependencies that make your timescale unrealistic.

Set a Goal That Excites and Motivates

Rather than a "negative" target (e.g. *reducing customer complaints*), express your goal as a positive (e.g. *getting great customer feedback*). This is more motivating and attracts you towards it. It's also helpful to visualise what it will be like when you have reached your target. What will you be doing? What will people be saying to you? How will you feel? Find ways to remind yourself of your goal – have a picture on your desk or an object to remind you. Imagine how good it will feel to succeed.

The Motivation Equation: $M = V \times D \times A$

To motivate yourself and others towards a goal, it can help if you have a **vision** of what you want to achieve, a feeling of

dissatisfaction with the current situation and some **actionable** first steps. For example, if I want to motivate myself to write a book, I need three things:

- A **vision** of myself holding the book in my hand and seeing it on display in a book shop – this vision attracts me towards it, acting as a pull to my motivation
- To feel **dissatisfied** with the lack of books that meet the needs of my coaching clients for specific practical guidance
- **Actionable first steps** – some small things to get started, such as interviewing leaders, with short-term measures of success that will sustain my motivation

Guide to Writing SMARTER Goals

People should be able to see how their own goals at work relate to and contribute to the overall objectives of the organisation – the "golden thread."

SPECIFIC – State exactly what you need to achieve, write it in the positive, and specify the outcome you want.

MEASURABLE – Identify a measure – how you will know you have achieved it? How would someone else know if you have achieved it?

ATTAINABLE – Plan the activity to make it attainable. Are the right resources and support in place?

REALISTIC – Check that it is realistic. Is it challenging enough but not unrealistic? What are the risks or dependencies that might throw the plan off course?

TIME-BOUND – Put a timescale or deadline in. Have you set a date by which you will achieve it?

EXCITING – What aspect excites you most? How does it tap into your top motivator?

REWARDED – What type of recognition would you appreciate when you achieve this goal?

Try out these principles on a work-related goal for yourself or follow this template to set a goal with one of your team members.

Specific	*What Is My Goal?*
Measurable	How will I know I've achieved my goal? What will I see, hear, think, and feel that tells me I have got it?
Attainable	What are my first steps? What are the dependencies? What resources are needed?
Realistic	What is my plan? What could go wrong? What contingency time should I build in?
Time-related	What is my timescale? What are the milestones?
Exciting	What will achieving this goal do for me? How will I feel when it is achieved?
Rewarded	How will I celebrate when I achieve this goal?

GIVING FEEDBACK THAT WORKS

Feedback is giving information on which someone can act, in response to something they have said or done.

In other words, feedback needs to be actionable. Telling someone that they *"did a great job"* is not feedback, as it is not information on which they can act. It is much more helpful to tell them *what* was good about what they did. For example, during a presentation, they might have been effective in how they engaged the audience, or answered questions, or structured their presentation, or explained key points.

Feedback is an essential part of learning, and when there is no feedback, people find it impossible to sustain good performance. People tend to focus their activity on what they are measured on and what they receive feedback on. If there is no measurement and no feedback, they tend to stop doing the activity, as they get the message that it is not important.

It is often said that you should give five times the amount of positive feedback as negative feedback. This is because we have a negativity bias and give more weight to negative comments. Too much negative feedback can undermine confidence. (NB: this does not mean that you should give positive feedback when someone is performing poorly.)

Barriers to Giving Feedback

We often shirk away from giving feedback. Even when it is positive, we tend to find it a bit embarrassing and awkward.

What stops us giving or asking for feedback?

- Fear of hearing something we don't want to hear, e.g. criticism
- Fear of how the person we want to give feedback to might react
- Lack of skill in receiving feedback in an open-minded, non-defensive way that leads to learning
- Lack of skill in giving feedback in a constructive, non-judgemental way that leads to a plan for improvement
- Embarrassment at giving or receiving praise

We are not very skilled at receiving feedback either. If someone tells us that we have done something well, we tend to pass over it and move on. But pausing to give or receive feedback is important. It helps us work out what we are good at as well as where we could improve. We take our own talents for granted and assume that everyone shares them. When someone tells us what we have done well, it increases our self-awareness and encourages us to do more of it.

We often make a distinction between positive feedback and constructive (or negative) feedback. Another distinction is between feedback which is **opinion** and feedback which is **observation**. It can be easier to give and receive observational feedback – this is simply an account of what somebody has done or said and the impact it had – whereas your opinion is your personal judgement of whether something was good or bad, and this can be disputed.

Principles for Giving Feedback

- Start with a positive if you can
- Be specific – what did they do or say?
- Give observations, not opinions
- Describe the impact of the behaviour (positive or negative)
- Offer advice
- Own the feedback – it must be your observations, not a report from someone else

The reason it's helpful to start with a positive is that the person will not feel threatened or become defensive, if they hear something good first. This enables them to be open to acknowledging where improvements can be made.

Guide to Giving Feedback

Here is a step-by-step model for giving feedback.

Individual shares	Step 1 *What they think they did well*	Step 3 *Ideas on what they would do differently*
Manager shares	Step 2 *What they think the individual did well*	Step 4 *Advice on what they could do differently*

If you regularly adopt this style of giving feedback to your team members, you will find that they start doing it in this format for themselves and you will be creating a learning culture in your team.

See also the Learning Cycle in Chapter 4.

There are times when you need to give more negative than positive feedback, because you want someone to change their behaviour or performance. The format below works well for this:

- What I would like you to stop doing (because it's not effective)
- What I would like you to start doing (in order to be more effective)
- What I would like you to carry on doing (because it's working well)

Try this out – think of one of your current team members, and note what you would like them to stop, start, or continue doing.

Stop doing	
Start doing	
Continue doing	

Giving feedback in this format works because it does not make people feel defensive, and it gives them clear guidance on your expectations. And it ends on a positive note.

COACHING TO BUILD SELF-BELIEF

If there were never any problems, we wouldn't need managers – problem-solving is part of a leader-manager's role, including solving people's problems. When our teams run into difficulties in their work, they expect their managers to be able to help them. There are two basic ways to help people:

- Either tell them what to do, or
- Coach them to work out what to do for themselves

These are both valid approaches and can be equally effective, depending on the situation. As a leader-manager, you need to be able to do both and to choose which is appropriate for the circumstances.

Each approach has consequences – positive and negative.

Telling people what to do can be helpful when:

- The employee is inexperienced and needs some specific guidance
- There is a crisis and no time for discussion
- There is a rule, procedure, or process that must be followed

Coaching people can be helpful when:

- You want them to take responsibility for their action
- There is no obvious single solution to a problem
- You want to build their confidence in their ability

Initially, it can seem quicker to tell people what to do rather than have a coaching conversation with them. However, it is possible to have short coaching conversations, and this way you build capability in your team, meaning that they need less support in the future.

As a manager, you have a choice about where you are on the spectrum below in any situation. Whenever you are in discussion with a team member, consider where you want to be (Figure 5.3).

PERSISTENCE AND PERFORMANCE **117**

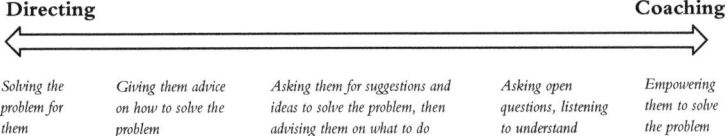

Directing				Coaching
Solving the problem for them	Giving them advice on how to solve the problem	Asking them for suggestions and ideas to solve the problem, then advising them on what to do	Asking open questions, listening to understand	Empowering them to solve the problem

Figure 5.3 Directing – Coaching Spectrum

What Is Coaching?

Coaching is not training, telling, or showing someone what to do. It is helping them, through asking open questions, to work out answers for themselves.

Here are some definitions of coaching:

> Unlocking a person's potential to maximise their own performance. It is helping them learn rather than teaching them[9]
> Supporting an employee, either as an individual, as part of a team and/or organization to achieve improved business performance and operational effectiveness[10]
> Helping someone to learn to solve a problem or do a task better than would otherwise have been done[11]
> The underlying intent of every coaching interaction is to build the coachee's self-belief[12]

The last quotation, from John Whitmore, captures the essence of what a coaching style of managing achieves – it builds "awareness, responsibility and self-belief." After a coaching conversation, people feel accountable for what they are going to do, and they feel confident in their ability to do it. And as we know, this confidence is a critical part of being persistent and motivated.

What follows is a brief overview of the core elements of coaching. Like any skill, it is best to learn it through attending a workshop where you can get practice and feedback.

Guide to Coaching

The GROW model is a framework for guiding your questions (Figure 5.4).

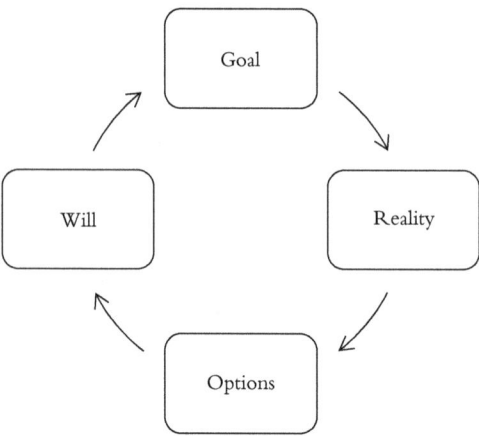

Figure 5.4 The GROW Model[13]

Establish the Goal

When a team member comes to you with a problem, the starting point is to establish what they want to achieve in relation to this problem – their goal.

In doing this, it is useful to ask questions like:

> What would you like to achieve with this issue?
> Where do you want to get to with this problem?
> What would your ideal outcome be?
> How will you know that you have achieved that goal?
> How will you know the problem is solved?

Examine Current Reality

Next, ask your team member to describe the current situation. This is a very important step as it helps ground them before exploring options. As the team member tells you about his or her current reality, they might start to see some solutions.

Useful coaching questions include:

> What is happening now?
> What, who, when, how often?

What is the impact of that?
What have you tried so far?
Who else is affected by this issue?

Explore the Options

Once your team member has described the current reality, you can move on to explore the many possible options for solving the problem. Help your team member generate as many good options as possible. Let them do most of the talking, and defer any suggestions of your own until later.

Typical questions to establish the options are:

What could you do to deal with this problem?
What else could you do?
What alternatives are there to that approach?
What if this or that constraint were removed?
How have other people dealt with similar problems?

Establish the Will

By examining current reality and exploring the options, your team member will now have a good idea of how they can achieve their goal. That's great – but in itself, this may not be enough! Your final step as coach is to ask your team member to commit to specific action. This turns ideas into concrete actions and commitment.

Useful questions:

What will you do now … and when?
What are the next steps you will take?
What could stop you moving forward?
How can you overcome any blockers?
What support do you need?

You may have noticed that almost all the questions above begin with *What* or *How*. These are non-threatening and open up the conversation, whereas questions beginning with *Why* tend to make people defensive and close down exploration of the options. Similarly, closed questions (e.g. questions beginning with *have you, will you, did you, can you*) also restrict thinking.

Sometimes towards the end of a coaching conversation, you may want to move along the spectrum away from coaching towards giving advice or direction.

At the end you may also like to ask your team member something like:

What was useful about the questions I asked you?

You might be pleasantly surprised at the response!

DOING IT VIRTUALLY

Setting goals, giving feedback, and coaching can be done virtually, and often are. In some ways, communicating virtually is not that different from in-person communication. In both cases, you need to think about what outcomes you want and how best to put your points across through your words, tone of voice, and body language. But there are differences too.

Here are some practical considerations which can impact the quality of the virtual conversation:

- Be aware of your environment – what others will see. How does it look? What impression does it give? You may want to use a virtual background
- Check your image of yourself. Position your camera at eye height so that you can look directly at it when speaking. Don't sit with a window or light source behind you. Have your device on a stable surface. Position any documents on your screen near to your camera so that you can look at them while still making as much eye contact as possible. Getting these housekeeping issues right shows respect for the other person and that you regard the conversation as important
- People sometimes think it is harder to pick up cues from others virtually, but because you are facing everyone directly, they may notice your facial expressions and your gestures. Be aware of the messages you are transmitting and any annoying habits you may have – they will notice them! When you communicate virtually, people usually see your face and top half of your body. Being able to see your hand gestures gives a more natural feeling to the communication

- You may need to make more effort to pick up other people's responses to you. It may be more difficult than in person to interpret how someone is reacting. You may need to ask them what they are thinking or feeling
- Be sensitive to the time of day for the other person – if you are in Europe and they are in Asia-Pacific, it may be the end of a long tiring day for them, so not the best time to discuss sensitive topics. There may be cultural aspects too, such as national or religious holidays that need to be respected
- Use language without jargon and slang, especially when talking with non-native speakers, and be aware of cultural references that may be meaningless to others
- Don't have back-to-back virtual meetings, as they can be very draining – and make sure the person you are talking to has a break between meetings too. If it is a long meeting, have a break after 45 minutes so you can both get up and move around

CREATING A CULTURE OF PERSISTENCE

Much of this chapter has been about how you can encourage your individual team members to persist by setting motivating goals, giving feedback that works, and coaching to build self-belief. There are also things you can do to encourage a culture of persistence in the whole team – one where people keep going despite difficulties and support and encourage each other. For example:

- Run reviews/lessons learned sessions for the whole team
- Involve the whole team in setting objectives and strategy
- Arrange for people to buddy up or mentor each other
- Encourage support and challenge behaviours in team meetings (see Chapter 4)
- Create opportunities for social connection
- Give recognition for effort and achievement to the whole team

TIPS FOR THE TOP MOTIVATORS

These three management practices – setting motivating goals, giving feedback that works, and coaching to build self-belief – have a big impact on how people think and feel about their work and therefore a big impact on how they sustain their motivation.

	Improviser (Freedom)	Stabiliser (Belonging)	Theorist (Competence)	Catalyst (Potential)
Goal setting They like goals which… They might need help to…	Are specific, practical. Short-term Fun Show immediate results Plan longer term Brainstorm other options	Are specific, practical. Planned with steps, timescales, and clear accountabilities Adjust the goals for changes Brainstorm other options	Include innovative approaches Lead to long-term change Engage other people in their vision Make it practical and feasible	Include creative approaches Make things better for people Think through the pros and cons Make it practical and feasible
Feedback They like feedback which…	Recognises they have made their mark and been impressive Is immediate	Recognises their efforts for the group and their results. Includes physical tokens (e.g. certificates, awards)	Recognises the high standard of their work and their ideas Comes from someone whose competence they respect	Recognises the harmony and insights they bring Is personal, authentic, and regular
Coaching They like coaching which is/ has…	In short sessions. A specific aim Practical output Focus on "how to…"	Clear goals and a plan An agenda for the session Focus on "what…"	Opportunity to brainstorm With someone they respect Focus on "why…"	Opportunity to share ideas With someone they trust Focus on "who…"

Positive self-talk Remind them of how they…	Adapt to circumstances Make an impact Get results Are appreciated by others for being fun	Fulfil their responsibilities Fit into the group and contribute Bring needed structure and consistency	Make achievements Are competent Share valuable knowledge and expertise	Help other people reach their aspirations Bring people together and create harmony
What helps them persist Advise them to…	Build in some fun elements or make it a contest Remember "what's in it for you" Have a visible and tangible way to demonstrate progress Create a physical environment that helps them feel good	Recall what has helped them to persist in the past Get ideas from others to solve the problem Use to-do lists as a plan of what to do and as a record of what they have done Find someone to take on some of their duties (if they want to)	Use mind mapping to capture ideas Focus on the goal and avoid being side-tracked Look for links to something that's important to them Find people whose expertise they respect to mentor them	Find a connection to a greater purpose Keep a log of three good things that happen each day Not take it personally when people disagree with their ideas Check out the practicality of their ideas with others

You can go further and tailor how you set goals, give feedback, and coach, to the top motivators of your team members. Here are some tips.

SUMMARY

Persistence is about how we keep ourselves motivated. It is about how we manage our thoughts, beliefs, and emotions to stay positive and confident.

How we think and feel has an enormous impact on our motivation. As a leader-manager, you influence – whether you intend to or not – what people think and feel by what **you** do and say. **Your** behaviour influences **their** thoughts and emotions, so it is important to be intentional about what you do and what you say.

Leader-managers can influence individual's persistence by how you set goals, give feedback, coach, and create a persistent culture in the team. These activities can be more challenging when team members are working remotely – see Chapters 6 and 7 for guidance on managing hybrid and global teams.

ACTION PLAN

- What are your key leaning points from this chapter?
- What do you plan to do differently with your team members?
- What do you need from your own manager?
- What helps you persist?

Actions for My Team	*Actions for Me*

NOTES

1 Gallwey, T. (2000). *The Inner Game of Work: Overcoming Mental Obstacles for Maximum Performance.* New York: Texere.
2 Oxford English Dictionary.
3 From Simon Mundie interview, "Don't tell me the score," broadcast on BBC Radio 4 on 1 November 2018.
4 Goffman, E. (1967). *The Presentation of Self in Everyday Life.* New York: Anchor Books.

5 Helen Bradley, Client Director, Executive Education, Imperial College Business School.
6 Zinsser, N. (2022). *The Confident Mind: A Battle-Tested Guide to Unshakeable Performance*. London: Cornerstone Press.
7 Sigal Barsade, Professor of Management, Wharton School, University of Pennsylvania, speaking on BBC Radio 4 "In the Balance – EI and Business," January 2014.
8 Locke, E. and Latham, G. (1990). *A Theory of Goal Setting & Task Performance*. Englewood Cliffs, NJ: Prentice Hall.
9 Gallwey, T. (2000). *The Inner Game of Work: Overcoming Mental Obstacles for Maximum Performance*. New York: Texere.
10 *Association for Coaching*.
11 Megginson, D. and Boydell, J. (1979). *A Manager's Guide to Coaching*. London: CIPD.
12 Whitmore, J. (2002). *Coaching for Performance*. 3rd edition. London: Nicholas Brealey.
13 Ibid.

HELPFUL HABITS AND RESILIENT BEHAVIOURS

INTRODUCTION

The third aspect of motivation – resilience – has a big impact on well-being (Figure 6.1). To create a resilient environment for your team, you must be resilient yourself. As you read this chapter, take the opportunity to reflect on how to manage your work and life to increase your own resilience. Apply the tips and tools to yourself, and become a role model for your team. This makes a sound basis for helping your team members build their own resilience. You will be better placed to help them develop helpful habits and behaviours to maintain their energy levels and deal more effectively with the things that drain their energy and cause them stress.

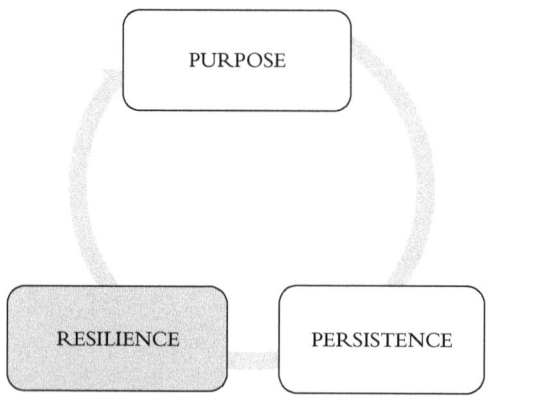

Figure 6.1 Motivation: Purpose, Persistence, and Resilience

DOI: 10.4324/9781003286646-7

Support from managers and colleagues is a strong predictor for how resilient a person is at work. Having positive relationships decreases work-related stress and provides psychological resources for coping.[1] One of my interviewees[2] describes how, during the first pandemic lockdown in 2020, he was aware that "as a leader, you can't portray panic," and he consciously projected a calm and reassuring manner. He also recognised that "people depend on each other," and so he encouraged people to talk to each other.

Leader-managers can create a resilient environment for their teams by listening and being empathic and by role modelling resilient habits and behaviours.

WHAT IS RESILIENCE?

Resilience is about how well we recover from setbacks and keep going towards achieving our goals rather than giving up. The dictionary definition[3] is *the ability to bounce back from the challenges and setbacks that life throws at us and maintain a positive outlook*. I see resilience as:

> Building physical, mental, and emotional energy to recover from setbacks and maintain momentum.

This quotation – "My barn having burned down, I can now see the moon" by Mizuta Masahide (17th-century Japanese poet and samurai) – shows extreme resilience – most of us would struggle to see the silver lining in that particular cloud. However, it illustrates that how we think about and reframe situations is important for resilience, just as it is for persistence. Resilience is also about energy.

ENERGY

Resilience comes from looking after all aspects of yourself – your body, mind, and spirit. Looking after your physical energy – by healthy eating, getting enough sleep, exercise, and fresh air – is as important for your resilience as looking after your mental, emotional, and spiritual energy (Figure 6.2).

Figure 6.2 Energy and Resilience

When we have energy at all these levels, we are more likely to feel motivated and be able to maintain momentum. We also have a greater sense of well-being too.

There are complex links between our brains and our bodies, and each affects the other. We can think or imagine things that cause a physical reaction. If you are nervous about something, such as a job interview, you may have butterflies in your stomach. If you imagine a lemon, saliva may be secreted into your mouth, even when you don't have a lemon in front of you. What we think in our heads can affect our bodies.

Similarly, what we sense in our bodies can affect what we think. If your stomach rumbles, you get the message that you are hungry and should get some food. If your face goes red, your brain rapidly tries to work out what the cause might be – are you angry, embarrassed, or just hot? Your brain draws conclusions based on the situation[4] – "your brain makes meaning from the identical situation in different ways, depending on the context" – then you decide the appropriate action to take.

When something happens, we have physical reactions (e.g. sweaty palms) as well as emotional reactions (e.g. feeling excited or tense). These links between brain and body, discovered by neuroscientists, have implications for how we motivate ourselves. It is not only about how we think: being resilient involves paying attention to your whole self – body (physical energy), mind (mental and emotional energy), and spirit (sense of purpose and meaning).

Body – Creating Healthy Habits

Looking after your physical needs for healthy food, exercise, fresh air, and rest is a strong foundation for resilience. Most of us have experienced situations where something that seemed very challenging when we were tired seem a lot less worrying after a good night's sleep. Going for a walk in nature is not only good for our bodies but is now proven as a mental health benefit too.[5]

Being resilient involves creating habits that sustain your motivation. For example, if I want to exercise more, then I need to make it easy to start and make it become part of my daily or weekly routine – I might put it in my diary, arrange to meet a friend, leave my kit by the front door, and go whatever the weather. It also helps to set small, achievable goals, such as running around the block, not doing a marathon!

Creating a habit means you do something on autopilot – you don't waste time and energy by stopping to think about whether you want to do it or how to do it. Of course, this applies to bad habits too, and it can take cognitive effort to change something that we do automatically.[6]

> *Hans* decided he wanted to limit the amount of time he was spending on emails. He tended to open emails as soon as they came in, interrupting what he was doing. He did this automatically without thinking about it. He realised that each time this happened, it took a while to get back into the work he had been doing, which was inefficient. He made a conscious decision to deal with emails only when he was having a coffee – usually around four times a day. Going to the coffee machine gave him a break and acted as a trigger for him to look at his emails when he returned to his desk, before resuming his work.

Mind – Being Mindful, Not Mind Full!

Techniques such as mindfulness enable you to become aware of what is happening in your body. If you can calm your body – for example by deep breathing – your mind and thoughts become calmer too – they help you to move forward rather than hindering you.

People who are high achievers tend to be very competitive against their own high standards and often put themselves under excessive pressure to do well at whatever they are doing. One of my interviewees[7] talks about "wanting to do well" and "not be found wanting" (often a sign of the Theorist motivation pattern). She describes how doing yoga helps to still her mind – it stops her continually thinking about what to do next. She also finds going for a run brings clarity to her thoughts and helps her prioritise.

Our mental energy fluctuates during the day, just as physical energy does. We get mentally tired – being in meetings, dealing with emails, writing reports, resolving problems, talking to people – all the normal day-to-day activities drain our energy. But energy can be replenished. How much do you build these things into your day to conserve and replenish your mental energy?

- Take a lunch break away from your workplace
- Take a walk outside once a day
- Get up from your desk at least once an hour
- Prioritise more effectively; watch the "urgent but not important" habit
- Reduce interruptions by carrying out high-concentration tasks away from phones and email
- Block out time in your diary for the important tasks
- Build in breaks between and after meetings
- Each night, identify the most important task for the next day, and do it first[8]

What new habits can you create? Which old ones can you eliminate?

Helpful Habits to Start	*Unhelpful Habits to Stop*

Emotional Energy

Our emotional energy also fluctuates during the day. The Talogy feelings wheel[9] illustrates the feelings we might experience at different times during a day. The top boxes relate to higher intensity feelings, while the bottom boxes relate to lower intensity feelings. The boxes on the right relate to positive feelings, while those on the left relate to negative feelings (Figure 6.3).

Figure 6.3 Emotional Energy

These are typical emotions experienced by people in each quadrant:

- Energise: excited, enthusiastic, happy, optimistic, engaged
- Stress: anxious, worried, irritable, angry, frustrated
- Burnout: depressed, drained, exhausted, hopeless
- Renew: calm, reflective, content, relaxed, interested

During the pandemic, people experienced record levels of worry, stress, anger, and sadness.[10] Being aware of your emotional energy means that you can take active steps to manage it.

You can enhance your resilience by doing the things that keep you on the right-hand side of the model so that you alternate between Energy and Renew. You can't be in Energise all the time – we all need downtime to recharge our batteries, but sometimes we don't allow ourselves to do that, and we eventually flip over into Stress. Being in the Stress box long term can have serious consequences for physical and mental health. Consider:

- What conditions are needed for you to be on the right-hand side?
- When do you feel energised? When do you feel renewed?

- What situations cause you to move to the left-hand side?
- How can you notice when you are moving to the left and do something about it?
- What can help you get back to Energise or Renew?

You can build your emotional energy with some simple practices:

- At the end of the day, write down three positive things that have happened
- Manage your mood – do something that cheers you up (listen to music, go for a walk, read, phone a friend)
- Let positive feedback from others sink in and make a note of it
- Spend quality time with family and friends

What can you do to build your emotional energy?

Building Emotional Energy

Looking after your physical, mental, and emotional needs is important to maintain your energy and build up your resources to deal with challenges and setbacks.

WHAT IS STRESS?

Stress occurs when we do not have enough resilience – physical, mental, and emotional energy – to cope with the challenges we face. The greater the challenge, the more resources we need. Stress is not an illness, but if it becomes excessive and prolonged, physical and mental illness can develop.

Most people experience stress at some time in their lives. Some pressure is essential to a healthy life. Too little pressure can lead to boredom and ill-health, while some pressure acts as a motivator and can help us achieve our goals and perform better, leading to better health.[11] Stress occurs when pressure becomes excessive.

The experience of stress is not the same for everyone – people differ in what situations they find stressful, how they react to them, and what helps them deal with it. In addition, if individuals do not get the opportunity at work to meet their core needs (i.e. needs for purpose, freedom, competence, belonging, fulfilling potential), that itself causes stress and leads to demotivation.

Research carried out by the UK Institute of Leadership and Management (ILM)[12] showed a direct correlation between a manager's happiness, their ability to cope with stress and workload, and their overall performance. According to the ILM:

> The ability to cope with stress and manage workload is a critical skill for successful managers.

Causes and Symptoms of Stress

According to the Chartered Institute of Personnel and Development's (CIPD)[13] report in 2021, **workloads remain by far the most common cause of stress at work, followed by management style**. The COVID-19 pandemic has created additional stressors. Relationships, at and outside work, are also commonly blamed for stress.

My coaching clients often cite too many emails, too much time lost in meetings, and too much to do in the time available as causes of stress. They often work at home in the evenings and weekends – which leads to more stress. Working in this way undermines all the core motivators – you don't have freedom to act, you feel incompetent, you don't get enough connection with others, and you can't fulfil your own potential or enable others to fulfil theirs.

Events in people's lives outside work may also cause stress. Major life events – serious illness, divorce, children leaving home, moving house – are obvious stressors. Events such as holidays and Christmas can also be stressful and have an impact on people's behaviour at work.

What happens to us outside work can affect our resilience and our motivation at work. This means that leader-managers who want to enable the motivation of their staff must be supportive towards personal problems and about issues such as work-life balance.

Anyone can suffer from work-related stress, no matter what work they do. Symptoms of stress might include any of the following:

Changes in Behaviour	Physical Symptoms	Mental Symptoms	Emotional Symptoms
You may: Find it hard to sleep Change your eating habits Smoke or drink more Avoid friends and family Drive recklessly Develop nervous tics Show OCD behaviours	Might include: Fast breathing Raised blood pressure Tiredness Indigestion and nausea Headaches Aching muscles Palpitations Panic attacks	You may: Become indecisive Find it hard to concentrate Suffer loss of memory Feel inadequate Have low self-esteem Lose self-confidence Make rash decisions Lose perspective	You may: Get irritable or angry Be anxious Feel numb Be hypersensitive Feel drained and listless Feel insecure Fear criticism Feel hopeless

What causes you stress? And what impact does it have on your behaviour and on the people around you?

Causes	Symptoms	Impact

When asked how they deal with stress, people are more likely to name sedentary and solitary activities, such as watching TV, surfing the net, listening to music, or reading a book, than active and group ones, even though more active strategies are proven to be more effective.

THE LEADER-MANAGER'S ROLE

Leader-managers and colleagues play critical roles in influencing how resilient people are. Research shows that there are a wide range of factors that predict resilience,[14] and some of them can be influenced by how people are managed. These include confidence in your own ability (as discussed in Chapter 5) and having social support, in the form of help or advice people at work. Support from colleagues is especially powerful, so encouraging a climate where people are willing to help each other is important.

To be resilient and stay motivated, people need to:

- Know how to look after their energy levels
- Be aware of and able to manage their emotional states
- Know how to reduce their causes of stress
- Be aware of techniques to manage their symptoms of stress

It can be tricky for managers to help individuals build resilience without appearing too intrusive, particularly if some of the causes of stress stem from their life outside work. But there is an expectation from employees that managers will be "empathic,"[15] and empathy is seen as a key characteristic of successful leaders. You will know which members of your team need this sort of support if you have good communication with them.

You can demonstrate both empathy and practical leadership in these ways:

- Listen to your team – know what is going on for them at work and outside work
- Role model resilient behaviours, and encourage people to support each other
- Build helpful habits in how you run the team
- Give advice and guidance on prioritising and dealing with the things that drain their energy

The next sections cover these aspects of leadership.

Listening

It is difficult to fully listen to somebody. We think we listen to other people, but often we are distracted by our own thoughts, or by the emails popping into our inbox or the pings on our phones, or what is happening around us. This does not make us good listeners, and

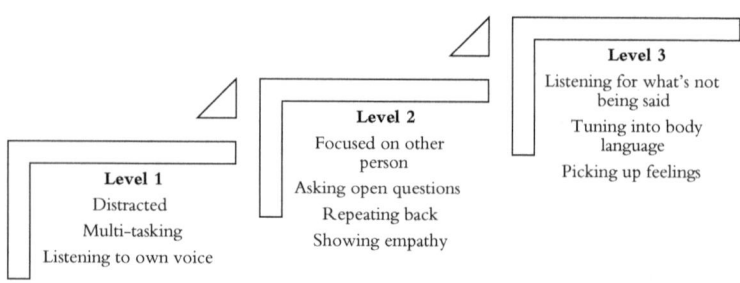

Figure 6.4 Levels of Listening

we may fail to pick up on important issues. Hearing is listening to what is said. Listening is hearing what is not being said.

We can listen at different levels (Figure 6.4).[16]

Level 1 listening is when you are distracted, tuned out, or thinking about other things. At level 2, you pay attention to the person, perhaps repeat back their own words and show curiosity by asking open questions (see section on coaching in Chapter 5). Level 3 listening is when you notice the non-verbal cues too – the body language, facial expressions, gestures, perhaps listening for what is not being said and picking up the underlying feelings about the issue.

As a leader-manager, you should know what is going on for your team members – this means creating opportunities to talk to them regularly, listen to them, and help them resolve problems affecting their work:

- Take time to do a bit of "managing by wandering around" (MBWA[17]), perhaps diarise some time each day
- If you or your team members are working partly or wholly from home, find creative ways to do MBWA – perhaps start a virtual "tea at three" chat, or a weekly lunch together
- Put one-to-one sessions in your calendar and give them priority – this sends the message that your team is important to you

What can you do to listen better to your team?

Moving Up the Levels of Listening

Role Modelling Resilient Behaviours

You create the culture in your team by what you do and what you say. People take their cue from you. Which of these could you tick?

	Tick
I make time to talk to people informally	
I take all my holidays each year	
I send emails at reasonable times of day, not late at night or at weekends	
I leave work on time at least twice a week	
I rarely eat lunch at my desk	
I disconnect from email when on holiday	
I spend time on activities which have long-term value	
I take regular breaks during the day to truly renew and recharge	
I take time to reflect on what has gone well each day	
I rarely work in the evenings or at weekends	
I take time to think and plan ahead at work	
I spend quality one-to-one time with my team members	
I rarely feel irritable, impatient, or anxious at work	
I deal effectively with conflict	
I give enough support to my team members	

How many items were you able to tick?

Check back on the section on Energy earlier in this chapter. Which behaviours to build physical, mental, and emotional energy do you or could you start to practice?

Resilient Behaviours

Building Helpful Habits

It is said that we need to repeat a behaviour many times for it to become a habit. One piece of research[18] concluded that it takes between 18 to 254 days for a person to form a new habit, with an average of 66 days for a new behaviour to become automatic.

The advantage of habits is that they take the thinking out – it's like putting on a seat belt when you get into a car; you do it without needing to think about it. Our brains like to reduce effort in this way. You can make life easier for yourself by building helpful habits into how you run your team. Consider the list below, and tick which items are common practice in your team.

	Tick
Arriving at meetings on time	
Starting and finishing meetings on time	
Building time into calendars before and after meetings	
Sending agendas in advance and expecting people to prepare	
Only copying people on emails who need to be copied	
Avoiding "reply all" responses	
No laptops or phones in meetings (unless needed for the purpose of the meeting)	
Disabling email when working on something important	
Setting aside specific times of the day to look at email	
Following the 4 D's when opening emails (do it, delete it, delegate it, or defer it)	
Speaking to someone rather than conducting debates by email	
Holding regular team meetings so people know who is doing what and who needs help	
Putting time in diaries for regular catch-ups and one-to-ones	

Some teams set out written ground rules so that the team runs smoothly and unnecessary conflict is avoided.

Of the items above that are **not** habits in your team (i.e. the ones you did not tick), which of these would you like to encourage? How could you communicate that to your team and get their buy-in?

Helpful Habits

Setting Priorities

One of the things that all my coaching clients struggle with is prioritising their workload. Stephen Covey's Urgent-Important Matrix[19] (adapted) is a useful tool to help you think about how you spend your time (Figure 6.5).

Take a big piece of flip chart paper, and draw the matrix on it. Think about all the typical activities you do in a week or a month, write each one on a post-it note, and then pin them on to the appropriate box.

Categorise them as follows:

1. **Fire-fighting** – things that are urgent and important and you constantly react to them – e.g. a customer complaint, a machine breakdown, a system failure
2. **False alarms** – things that seem urgent but may not be important – e.g. when someone says to you *"we've got a problem"* or *"we need a meeting"*
3. **Fire escapes** – things that are neither urgent nor important – e.g. doing emails before other more important tasks, surfing the net, getting distracted by other people's conversations
4. **Fire prevention** – things that are important but not urgent, so they tend not to get done, because we are too busy fire-fighting – e.g. putting processes in place to prevent problems, or working out long-term vision and strategy

Figure 6.5 Urgent and Important Matrix

How much of your time is spent on the activities that fall into each box? Do you spend enough time on the important, preventive, strategic activities?

If we spent more time on fire prevention, there would be less fire-fighting to do, and most of us would feel happier at work – except possibly for the Improvisers, who may genuinely love a crisis!

Fire prevention often seems like it is "too hard." It is sometimes easier to be reactive and deal with each crisis as it arises rather than making time to think longer term and put permanent corrective actions in place.

Once you have categorised your post-its, you can identify which ones you should continue to DO and which you can DELETE or DELEGATE.

Resilience When Remote

Since the COVID-19 pandemic, there has been a permanent change to more flexibility in where and when you work, at least for office workers. Leader-managers will most likely always have some of their team members who do not appear every day in the office, and they may work remotely themselves some of the time too. It means that more discipline is required to make time to talk to all team members – including how to replicate those informal, water cooler chats that often lead to important outcomes.

It also means that you need to find ways to enable colleagues to connect with each other to strengthen their social ties, share ideas, and give encouragement to each other. Maybe you have an end-of-the-week virtual get-together, and rotate responsibility for organising it.

Checking in on the welfare of people working from home is important so that support can be provided if needed. The experience of lockdowns has shown that some people find it particularly difficult to work from home and, if forced to do so, may struggle to maintain their motivation and performance. Keep in regular contact so you can pick up quickly on any issues.

TIPS FOR THE TOP MOTIVATORS

There are specific stressors which affect people with different motivation patterns. Check out your own stressors and what can help. Which ones work for you? Which ones might help colleagues?

	What Stresses Them	Behaviour Under Stress	What Helps Them
Improviser need for freedom	Not seeing immediate results Being confined by rules Having to wait. Lack of information Feeling trapped and bored	Go their own way Disregard rules Ignore commitments Escalate the situation Retaliate	Bring some risk and fun into the mix Remove distractions and find a task to do Crafting something that other people see Physical activity, exercise, playing guitar Taking a break to focus on an activity-based hobby Being in a pleasing environment, looking at a view Having the opportunity to perform Having fun and being challenged People giving them a nice surprise Being given a practical problem to solve Having an exciting new activity
Stabiliser need for belonging	Not being able to contribute Constant changes of plan Not being recognised for their contribution Instability and ambiguity Feeling left out	Become dogmatic Try to control others Complain that they are not appreciated Blame others	Get things out of your head and on to lists Stick to the schedule, and plan in some fun time Being given responsibility and a role in the team Others providing order and structure People helping them to relax and to set limits Doing a visible activity with a purpose (e.g. repairing something) Finding someone else who can be trusted to take on the responsibility Being given a tangible reward or verbal or written praise that acknowledges their contribution Feeling needed and receiving appreciation Being included in a new group or activities with others

(Continued)

	What Stresses Them	Behaviour Under Stress	What Helps Them
Theorist need for competence	Feeling incompetent Lack of independence Routine and repetitive demands Detailed work with no reason	Become intolerant Engage in pedantic debate Become preoccupied with minute details Avoid people	Reading a book Learning something new with a purpose Someone helping them work out how to find the time for what they want to do Finding ways to reduce the routine and repetitive activities Someone making it ok for them to ask for help Getting positive feedback about their ideas Having a complex problem to think about Having some time free of demands to use as they want Teaching someone else something Achieving something important to them
Catalyst need to fulfil potential	Lack of positive feedback Doing work with no meaning Feeling insignificant Impersonal environment where people don't matter Conflict and criticism	Become self-sacrificing Become cynical about motives Pretend to go along with others Disconnect from others	Face-to-face contact and positive feedback to give them the sense of connection Having meaningful relationships Having a new role to develop potential People listening to their concerns Being nurtured by others Having an opportunity to help someone be happier Getting positive personal feedback and appreciation Finding something to be passionate about Spending time with loved ones Writing down what they could share with others Looking at reality rather than generalising Doing a creative activity

Adapted from Applications of the Survival Strategies Model, 2017, course presented by Eve Delunas, PhD, and Susan Nash.

SUMMARY

Resilience is about how well we recover from setbacks and keep going towards achieving our goals rather than giving up. Resilience comes from looking after all aspects of yourself in a holistic way and building your resources of physical, mental, and emotional energy.

Stress occurs when we do not have enough resilience – physical, mental, and emotional energy – to cope with the challenges we face. The greater the challenge, the more resources of energy we need. Stress can lead to changes in behaviour and may have physical, mental, and emotional symptoms.

Support from managers and colleagues is one of the main predictors of how resilient people are at work. Therefore, leader-managers need to both provide support and create an environment in which people support each other. They can also role model and instil resilient habits and behaviours in how the team operates. As workload is often cited as the main source of stress, leader-managers should ensure that workload matches capacity and build skills and confidence in prioritising.

ACTION PLAN

Look back over the notes you have made in this chapter.

What specific actions will you take to build resilient behaviours and helpful habits and to reduce stressors – both for yourself and for your team?

Actions for Me Personally	*Actions for My Team*

NOTES

1. Gifford, J. and Young, J. (2021). *Employee Resilience: An Evidence Review.* Summary report. London: Chartered Institute of Personnel and Development.
2. Ashley Oates, Market Area Director (Audi), Jardine Motors Group.

3. Oxford English Dictionary.
4. Barrett, L. (2018). *How Emotions Are Made: The Secret Life of the Brain.* London: Pan Books.
5. Friedman, L. F. and Loria, K. (2016). "11 Scientific Reasons you should be spending more time outside." *Business Insider UK.*
6. Kahneman, D. (2012). *Thinking Fast and Slow.* New York: Farrar, Straus and Giroux.
7. Helen Bradley, Client Director, Executive Education, Imperial College Business School.
8. Tracy, B. (2013). *Eat that Frog: Get More of the Important Things Done Today.* London: Hodder.
9. Talogy feelings wheel based on Russell, J. (1980). "A Circumplex Model of Affect." *Journal of Personality and Social Psychology* Vol. 39, No. 6, 1161–1178.
10. Gallup State of the Global Workplace 2021.
11. Yerkes, R. and Dodson, J. (1908). "The Relation of Strength of Stimulus to Rapidity of Habit-formation." *Journal of Comparative Neurology and Psychology* Vol. 18, No. 5, 459–482.
12. The pursuit of happiness: positivity and performance among UK managers, Institute of Leadership and Management 2012.
13. CIPD. (2021). *Health and Wellbeing at Work Survey 2021.* London: Chartered Institute of Personnel and Development.
14. Gifford, J. and Young, J. (2021) *Employee Resilience: An Evidence Review.* Summary report. London: Chartered Institute of Personnel and Development.
15. Hougaard, R., Carter, J., and Afton, M. (2021). "Connect with Empathy, but Lead with Compassion." *Harvard Business Review Press 2022.*
16. Adapted from Kimsey-House, H., Kimsey-House, K., Sandahl, P. and Whitworth, L. (2018) *Co-Active Coaching.* London: John Murray Press.
17. Peters, T. J. and Waterman, R. H. (1982). *In Search of Excellence: Lessons from America's Best-Run Companies.* New York: Harper & Row.
18. Lally, P., Jaarsveld, C., Potts, H., and Wardle, J. (2010). "How Are Habits Formed: Modelling Habit Formation in the Real World." *European Journal of Social Psychology* Vol. 40, 998–1009.
19. Covey, S. R. (1989). *The 7 Habits of Highly Effective People.* New York: Free Press.

UP CLOSE AND PERSONAL – LEADING AND WORKING WITH OTHERS

INTRODUCTION

How you lead and work with others is influenced by your own core motivator. People with different core motivators like to be led in different ways. In this chapter, you will look at the leadership style that comes naturally to you and how to consciously flex your approach to empower your colleagues to harness their own motivation.

The chapter also covers the impact of personality differences on styles of engaging and connecting and how these differences can lead to misunderstanding and conflict. There are sections on:

- Running effective meetings – including virtually
- Dealing with conflict
- Having difficult conversations
- Connecting with different people

You will consider your own development as a leader-manager and put together an action plan for enabling motivation in yourself and in your team.

LEADERSHIP STYLES

There are many models to describe leadership style. Any model should increase your awareness of the options available to you for flexing your style depending on the people and the circumstances.

Here we are looking at how your own motivation pattern and personality drive your behaviour as a leader. This is your starting point – being aware of what comes naturally to you means you can

DOI: 10.4324/9781003286646-8

146 LEADING AND WORKING WITH OTHERS

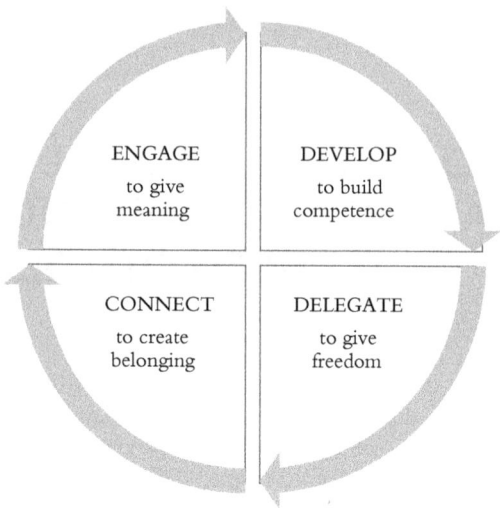

Figure 7.1 Leading Your Team to Fulfil Their Purpose and Potential

best use your talents. Being aware of how other people are motivated differently means you can adapt your approach to them, so they can use their talents and fulfil their potential. You will empower a more diverse team of people with a wider range of skills and perspectives.[1]

> To achieve group wisdom, you need wise individuals. But you also need diverse individuals, otherwise they will share the same blind spots.[2] *Matthew Syed*

The four key management capabilities for leading your team are shown in Figure 7.1. These tap into the core motivators.

What Are You Like as a Leader?

Your own top motivator gives a particular flavour and style to your leadership. It influences what you see as your priorities and how you choose to spend your time. If you do not have enough opportunity at work to tap into your own top motivator, you will not feel satisfied or fulfil your potential.

Look at the column that best reflects your motivation pattern – which points are generally true for you?

	Improviser	Stabiliser	Theorist	Catalyst
Motivated by	Freedom	Belonging	Competence	Potential
Strengths as a leader	Tactics Troubleshooting Dealing with present reality Creating excitement Assessing context	Logistics Planning Practical implementation Drawing on experience Creating stability	Strategy Innovation Long-term vision Systems thinking Building expertise	Diplomacy Developing people Appreciating others Sensitivity to climate
Weaknesses as a leader	Diplomacy Remembering commitments Reading long documents Following procedures	Strategy Deciding too early Seeing a way forward Appreciating others	Logistics Maintaining procedures Appreciating others Reality checking possibilities	Tactics Dwelling on negative events Wanting to please everyone Needing approval
Expects others to…	React quickly Be practical Know what's happening Be motivated by being in the action	Make a plan Be realistic Work hard Be motivated by responsibility	Have ideas Be independent Focus on the task Be motivated by achievements	Use imagination Be kind Work in harmony with others Be motivated by praise

Credit to Rowan Bayne.[3]

There are two important implications here:

1. High performance in any field comes from continual practice. We practise most what we are interested in and enjoy. We get better at those things – they become our signature strengths. Therefore, it is essential to have enough opportunity to spend time on the things we are interested in and enjoy, as this leads to high performance
2. Our own top motivator has a strong influence on what we expect of others. We see the world through our own lenses, our own motivators. We assume that what motivates us is what does – or should – motivate others. We then judge others against how much like us they are. We fail to spot their strengths and criticise them for their weaknesses

Looking at the three sections in the table above, and bearing these points in mind, what can you take from them? Here are some questions to aid your thinking.

Your Strengths

- How are you using your strengths in your current role – and are they having enough impact?
- What other opportunities could there be to apply your strengths?
- What does your own boss expect from you, and how far does this align with how you see your role and your best contribution?
- Consider the strengths that come naturally to people with the other three motivation patterns – which ones (if any) would you like to develop?

Building on My Strengths

Your Possible Weaknesses

- What impact do your weaknesses have on your performance – and how could you change that?
- How can you remind yourself to do the things you tend to ignore?
- How could you fill the gaps by involving people in your team?
- What could you delegate?

Minimising My Weaknesses

Your Expectations of Others

- How far do your expectations of your team members align with **their** motivators and strengths rather than yours?
- How could you create opportunities for them to use their own strengths?
- How fairly do you appraise them on what they can best bring?
- What could you do to fit the job to the person rather than the person to the job?

My Expectations of Others

Kate is in her late 20s and was recently appointed as a Head of HR for a high-tech manufacturing business. She is a member of the management team and has three HR professionals (all in their 40s) reporting to her plus an admin team. She is a Theorist with a vision of what an HR function should look like – she wants to move it from being reactive to more strategic. She gets frustrated by one of her team members who comes into work each morning, with no plan of what to do, and waits to see what comes up each day. She wants him to be more like her – to have longer-term goals and a plan for what he wants to achieve at work. This recently led her to downgrade his performance at the last review. During the conversation she realised that his performance was not bad but just different from what she would ideally like – he probably has the Improviser motivation. Together they agreed to reshape his role and how she delegated to him, to better reflect what he was good at and enjoyed.

Engaging Your Team – How Do They Like to Be Led?

We tend to give to others what we need ourselves instead of what *they* need. Here is what your team members might need from you, depending on their own top motivator.

	Improviser	Stabiliser	Theorist	Catalyst
Motivated by	Freedom	Belonging	Competence	Potential
Want to be valued for...	How they work. Dealing with a crisis	What they produce Getting things done	Their ideas Finding better ways to do things	Who they are Making a difference for people
Respond well to...	An informal approach A plan of action and short-term deadlines Compliments on using their initiative Praise for their results	A structured approach Clarity about the steps and timescales Compliments on their strong work ethic Checking in to confirm progress	Theoretically sound ideas Being asked about their opinion Compliments on their expert knowledge Being allowed independence	A warm personal approach Working collaboratively Compliments on their unique contribution Gratitude for their efforts
Don't respond so well to...	Rules and procedures Waiting for decisions Feeling controlled by rules or others	Unclear tasks or expectations Others dismissing their concerns Feeling their reliability is in doubt	Being told how to do their job Negative feedback Feeling their competence is questioned.	A business-like approach Criticism delivered bluntly Feeling their authenticity is undervalued
Do say...	*This is what you can do now...*	*This is the proof it will work...*	*This is how it will be more effective...*	*This is how it will be better for people...*
Don't say...	*Wait while we decide what to do...*	*It's an experiment, let's see what happens...*	*We will stick with what we know...*	*It doesn't matter what people think...*

Managers who are most successful at engaging and inspiring their team members are the ones who can adapt their communication to what works best with each individual. Bear in mind that what works best for each person will also:

- be influenced by their personal circumstances at the time
- vary as their personal circumstances change

Identify a couple of individuals in your team:

- Where are the potential mismatches between what you give and what they respond best to?
- How could you adapt your leadership style to do more of what they respond best to?

Mismatches

Having a conversation is the best way to find out what your team members need from you. You can ask them for feedback on:

- Which aspects of your management style work well for them?
- Which ones would they like you to change?

The Stop-Start-Continue template works well for this conversation (see Chapter 5). You might also consider thinking about this in relation to your own manager.

ENGAGING AND CONNECTING WITH YOUR TEAM

There is often a gap between our intention when we communicate and the actual impact of our communication on others (see Chapter 4), and then we do not have the influence that we want. Here are some ways to close the gap.

Matching the *style* of the person with whom we are communicating is one way to build rapport with them and bridge the gap.

- This includes adapting to whether they have a more **extraverted** or a more **introverted** style – their energy bias

Another way to create connection when you communicate is through the *content* of the communication.

- Some people pay more attention to **realistic, fact-based content**, while others prefer more **conceptual and ideas-based content** – their information bias

The consequences of these two sets of differences – energy bias and information bias – are covered below, in the context of running meetings.

Communication in Meetings

Managers spend half their time in meetings,[4] and in many organisations, they rush from meeting to meeting, grabbing a few moments in between to deal with the emails piling up in their inboxes, and with little time to do the work they are really paid to do, or to carry out the actions they have just picked up at the last meeting.

Meetings, whether virtual or in person, are a useful way of communicating with people, but they are not always effective. At the heart of a meeting is its *purpose*, but this will only be achieved if attention is paid to the *processes* and the *personalities* in the meeting (Figure 7.2).

Use my three Ps model to work out how to improve your meetings:

- Purpose – what is the meeting for?
- Processes – how will the meeting be run?
- Personalities – how will we behave towards each other?

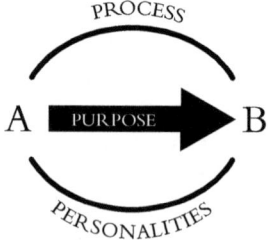

Figure 7.2 The Three Ps Model of Effective Teamwork

Purpose

Meetings are called for all sorts of reasons, which are not always obvious to the participants, so make sure you and they **know the purpose of the meeting** – is it to share information, analyse a problem, find a solution, build the team, make a decision, come up with an action plan? When you are at the meeting, keep the purpose in mind – it's easy to get side-tracked and forget what you are there for.

If you are invited to a meeting, **check that you need to be there**. Maybe there is another way that you can give or receive input? Or maybe you only need to be there for part of the time. Don't go along because of FOMO (fear of missing out)!

Processes

Follow the basics of good meeting practice – set an agenda, send out documents in advance (and read them), keep to time, note actions, follow up after the meeting, and so on. You might want to experiment with more radical approaches, such as banning PowerPoint, holding meetings standing up, and removing mobile phones. If meetings are virtual, make them short, have breaks, avoid distractions, and find ways to engage people (see Chapters 5 and 6 for more tips).

Depending on the purpose of the meeting, agree **effective processes** to achieve it – if the purpose of the meeting is to make a decision, what is the process for making it, who will be consulted, and whose voice will have most weight?

Having the purpose and processes clear are the basics for good meetings. But, provided these are in place, what really makes a difference to the effectiveness of meetings is not so much the mechanics of *running* meetings, but how people *participate* in them, and this is in part influenced by their personalities.

Personalities – Energy Bias

One of the most noticeable differences between people is whether they have a more extraverted or a more introverted style of communication. These terms were created by Carl Jung and refer to where you get your energy from and where you focus your energy – either on the external world of people and things or on the internal world of your own thoughts and feelings. We all need some time alone and some time with others, but the balance between the two varies from person to person.

In meetings, the people who have a bias towards extraversion tend to speak as they are thinking and have a faster pace, while people with a bias towards introversion tend to think first before speaking and have a slower pace. When there is a mix of people in a meeting, this can sometimes mean that the former may dominate the conversation and move on to other topics before the others have had a chance to share their thoughts and ideas. When most people in a meeting have the extraversion bias, there may be a lot of talking over each other and not listening, making it impossible for quieter people to get in. Conversely, if the participants mainly have the introversion bias, the meeting may be very quiet and lacking in energy, and anyone who is more extraverted may feel intimidated into silence.

Being aware of this difference means you can take some simple steps to ensure all views are heard and people are involved by adapting your own approach (Figure 7.3).

Figure 7.3 Extraverted and Introverted Communication

To help more extraverted colleagues, you can:

- Ask them for their opinions
- Allow time for them to talk so they can clarify their thinking
- Explain that others need some quiet time to think
- Speak briskly and respond quickly
- Project enthusiasm and be animated

To help more introverted colleagues you can:

- Send out an agenda and any pre-reading in advance
- Go round the room to ask for everyone's views in turn
- Take time out of the meeting to create some thinking time
- Have a calm tone and body language
- Don't interrupt when they are speaking

Personalities – Information Bias

People differ in the sort of information they pay attention to and trust, and this leads to difficulties in finding mutual understanding. Improvisers and Stabilisers tend to attend more to facts and information about present reality or the past, while the tendency of Theorists and Catalysts is towards ideas and possibilities for the future. Typically, when a group of people meet to discuss and decide on a topic, they focus on different aspects, because their minds work in different ways.

This is what they might be interested in:

Improvisers – Freedom	**Stabilisers – Belonging**
What are the facts?	What are the facts?
What is happening now?	What has happened already?
What can I get started on?	What have we done in the past on similar issues?
LET'S GO!	LET'S PLAN!
Theorists – Competence	**Catalysts – Potential**
What are the options?	What are the options?
What is our vision?	What is our vision?
What would work best?	What would help people most?
LET'S INVESTIGATE!	LET'S EVOLVE!

The questions each person asks shows what they naturally think about first. You can see there is a potential mismatch between the different groups. Stabilisers may be seen as too focused on the past, Improvisers as too hasty to rush ahead, Theorists too keen to redesign a whole system, and Catalysts as too idealistic. Stabilisers and Improvisers may be seen by their colleagues as lacking in imagination and Theorists and Catalysts may be perceived as ungrounded.

In meetings, this difference can quickly escalate into misunderstanding as people get frustrated with others who don't place importance on the same information as they do. In practice, this means that you should consciously ensure that all types of information – realistic, fact-based content, AND conceptual and people-oriented content – are explored during your meetings; otherwise, some participants will disengage, and the potential value of their input may be lost.

> A management team was considering relocating their office to a new business park 20 miles away. The managers mainly had the Stabiliser and Theorist motivation patterns, and they spent long meetings gathering information and discussing and weighing up the options. Finally, they made the decision to relocate and started to plan the details. However, they forgot to consider how their employees would be affected by the relocation and how they might react to the news. Had there been a Catalyst on the team, they might have considered this sooner and built in time to consult with employees.

What changes could you make to your meetings to make them more effective? Review all three Ps – Purpose, Processes, and Personalities.

Applying the Three Ps

Dealing with Disruptive Behaviours

Apart from personality differences, there are other behaviours that can sabotage both virtual and in-person meetings – people turning up late, not contributing, criticising colleagues, making unhelpful remarks, working on their laptops, looking at their phones, being defensive. As a result, participants leave meetings feeling frustrated and drained rather than motivated and energised. What can you do to improve the behaviours in meetings?

- As a team, discuss and **agree ground rules for behaviours** and meeting etiquette – typically, these include no laptops or phones, listening to each other, not talking over each other, showing respect for each other's opinions, confidentiality
- Pay attention to **tone of voice, facial expressions, and body language** – yours and theirs – so that you ensure you are sending the right messages and you pick up cues from others about what they might be thinking and feeling
- **Balance advocacy** (promoting your own position) **with enquiry** (finding out about theirs), and encourage others to do the same. This means explaining thinking, giving examples, sharing reasoning, seeking views, probing thinking, and encouraging challenge
- Approach meetings with a **"Do and Review" mindset**. After a meeting, take a few moments to reflect on what went well and what could have gone better. What could you do differently next time?

Virtual Meetings

The growth of virtual meetings during the COVID-19 pandemic has brought particular challenges.

- Online meetings are more intense – we have to concentrate harder, the cognitive demands are greater, and we get more tired. We need to make them shorter and less frequent
- There is less opportunity for side conversations and for bridge-building chats – everyone hears everything, and it feels more formal. You might need to make a special effort to schedule some one-to-one conversations – or go into breakout groups or use the chat function
- Everyone faces you (unlike in a real meeting), so you notice people's reactions immediately – who is looking interested or

bored, who is doing something else – but you may interpret their reactions incorrectly, and there is little opportunity to check this out
- You take it in turns to talk. This is good for more introverted people, who naturally assume that you take turns in conversation and like to think first before they speak. But it doesn't work so well for more extraverted people who tend to think as they speak and want to talk things out immediately rather than wait their turn. Encourage them to use the chat function instead
- You cannot do MBWA[5] (managing by wandering around) from home – you need to find other ways of virtually bumping into people and having water-cooler chats. Try a daily "Tea at three" session with your team
- Some people don't have their camera on – this makes rapport and collaboration harder. Set some ground rules and expectations around tech etiquette
- Set an expectation for the maximum number of hours someone should be in virtual meetings in a day

Despite these difficulties, there are also opportunities to reinvent how we do our meetings.

- Have fewer meetings! After all, going to meetings is not your work – you do most of your work outside the meetings. Challenge yourself to find other ways to discuss, decide, and communicate, without calling meetings
- Build personal relationships with your team members by having one-to-one chats with them, so you can find out what support they need
- Collaborative tools can work better virtually than in person – it's easier to see what others have written on their Post-its, easier to group common themes, and easier to build on other people's ideas
- It's easy to schedule comfort breaks into online meetings and less likely that people will get waylaid and won't come back after the break. And physically moving around aids concentration. Aim for a 30-minute break in between online meetings if they last more than 45 minutes

- Many office workers eat lunch at their desks while working – working from home may mean you can eat outside or with your partner and have a real break from work
- The chat function enables people to communicate without disrupting the meeting (especially useful for extraverts). The chat or whiteboard function is also a quick way to capture thoughts and ideas – faster than writing it on a real whiteboard
- It's easy to share documents and slides, and you can edit them as you present

TIPS FOR THE TOP MOTIVATORS – CONNECTING

We tend to communicate in a way that naturally fits our motivation pattern (see Chapter 3), so it is not difficult for us to "speak" to the people who share our pattern. But we may need to adapt our communication to build connection with people who have different motivation patterns.

Here are some tips:

Motivation Pattern	*How to Communicate with Them*	*Avoid*
Improviser	Be brief and specific Use an informal, casual, easy-going style Inject some fun or humour Focus on the present and the facts Set out clear expectations Show the immediate benefits of your proposals Set short-term deadlines rather than long-term goals Show how it makes life easier Allow them flexibility in how to achieve targets Words such as "simple," "effective," "proven," and "easy" tend to appeal to them	Being formal Making them feel controlled Talking too much about long-term plans and the big picture Lengthy emails and long reports – they are unlikely to read them Long meetings – they will check out Making them feel trapped or bored Giving them unwanted structure Ignoring their contribution Pausing before responding

Motivation Pattern	How to Communicate with Them	Avoid
Stabiliser	Give them a point of reference to your topic e.g. *"about the latest order…"* Provide facts and details. Proceed step by step in a logical fashion Give evidence and practical benefits Be respectful Establish clear next steps and actions Show confidence in their reliability Ask them what you can do to help them If you haven't worked out all the details, tell them this upfront Words such as "safe," "reliable," "proven," and "process" tend to appeal to them	Too much focus on the long-term future Unclear objectives Changes to the plan without evidence of need Vagueness and ambiguity Open-ended questions Questioning their reliability Giving too much information Leaving loose ends
Theorist	Give the overall picture first with a few relevant details Get down to business quickly Ask open-ended questions Make it a two-way conversation, not a monologue Explain the logic and the pros and cons Describe the long-term benefits Show confidence in their competence Expect to be challenged Ask for their ideas Words such as "innovative," "intelligent," "advanced," and "logical" tend to appeal to them	Giving lots of details verbally – they will only remember the few that interest them Talking **at** them rather than with them Questioning their competence Getting upset if they challenge your thinking Giving them negative feedback without clear justification Giving them positive feedback before they have finished – they won't value it

Motivation Pattern	How to Communicate with Them	Avoid
Catalyst	Give the overall vision first with a few relevant details Focus on how it will make a difference for people Ask open-ended questions Connect with them in an authentic way Be courteous and friendly towards them Give them opportunities to help others in creative ways Ask for their ideas Give them positive feedback and encouragement Show you care about the topic and about people's aspirations Words such as "compelling," "authentic," and "lasting impact" tend to appeal to them	Being blunt Intense debate or argument Asking them too many "why?" questions that seem to challenge them Focusing on the details Questioning their creativity Questioning their values Appearing not to care about people Framing "passionate" as "needy"

Credit to David Hodgson.[6]

DEALING WITH CONFLICT

When conflict blows up "out of nowhere" and escalates quickly, it is usually because someone's values have been infringed. We refer to "hitting a nerve" or "pressing a hot button." When our values are called into question, we feel threatened and react emotionally with the fight or flight response. The more primitive part of the brain (the amygdala and limbic system) kicks in first before the more rational part (the prefrontal cortex) can give a more considered response.

There are some specific trigger points for conflict between people based on their different motivation patterns. We have a deep attachment to what we value most. When someone else behaves in a way that appears to challenge or attack what we think is important, this can trigger an emotional reaction.

For example, if one of my values is being reliable, I am likely to react defensively if someone appears to suggest that I am not reliable. Similarly, if I have a high need to be competent, I will feel undermined when people point out things that I could have done better.

> *Josh* is a project manager in a water utility company and has the Stabiliser temperament. He's well suited to his role, has strong technical and planning skills, and is a diligent manager. He prides himself on meeting deadlines. However, he feels that one of his team, *Leann*, does not react quickly enough to requests. When he asks for progress reports, she tells him that it's all in hand but doesn't give him the evidence he wants nor show a sense of urgency. Leann, who has the Theorist pattern, hates having her competence questioned in this way and reacts by telling him to relax, which winds him up even more.

Anecdotally, there seems to be a higher incidence of conflict between people with the Stabiliser and Theorist motivation patterns. One reason could be that people with the Catalyst pattern are naturally more diplomatic and better able to avoid conflict. Another could be that both Stabilisers and Theorists tend to be task-focused, and some may not pay enough attention to nurturing relationships.

People with the Stabiliser motivation pattern value tradition, stability, and consistency, while people with the Theorist motivation pattern value new ideas, innovation, and change. There is clearly the potential for conflict between their different mindsets and approaches.

The key to avoiding conflict is to avoid triggering negative emotions by appearing to question their core values.

- For a Stabiliser, this means avoid suggesting that they are unreliable or are failing in their duty in some way
- For a Theorist, avoid suggesting that they are incompetent or have overlooked something important
- For an Improviser, avoid suggesting that they are unimpressive or lack impact
- For a Catalyst, avoid suggesting that they are too idealistic or too trusting in human nature

People value very distinct and different things. We need to tread carefully around people's values as we can inadvertently strike at the very heart of who they believe they are, their sense of self and identity.

Here are some of the values underpinning each motivation pattern and what can trigger a negative reaction:

Motivation Pattern	Values Include	Negative Triggers
Improviser	Freedom Action Fun Adaptability	Feeling constrained by rules Hierarchy Boredom – a lot of routine activities Feeling trapped
Stabiliser	Duty Responsibility Consistency Stability	Questioning their reliability Lack of respect for authority Lack of organisation Ignoring tradition
Theorist	Competence Independence Achievement Mastery	Telling them how they should do something Being told what to think Questioning their competence Feeling powerless
Catalyst	Uniqueness Authenticity Harmony Growth	People being insincere Behaviour causing disharmony Unethical behaviour Betrayal

Like giving presents at Christmas, we tend to give to people what we would like for ourselves, but a better approach is to give others what *they* need.

> **Susie** has the Theorist pattern and likes to be independent. When she was promoted to a management position, she gave her team members broad goals and expected them to work out for themselves how to achieve them – this is the style she preferred from her own manager. But this did not work for some of her team members. **Danny**, a Stabiliser, felt that she was making life hard for him by not telling him what steps to take to get started. He didn't see the point of reinventing the wheel. With experience, Susie learned who in her team benefited from more detailed instruction and who liked to be left alone to work it out for themselves.

Steps for Managing Conflict

When people feel threatened, they react emotionally rather than rationally. They become defensive and push their own point of view harder,[7] becoming more entrenched in their position and less willing to consider other perspectives. It's hard to resolve conflict when people are in the grip of emotion, so:

Step 1 is always to de-escalate. You can do this by:

- Taking a few minutes out – go to the coffee machine
- Moving to a different location – walk to a meeting room
- Using a quiet tone of voice and calm body language
- Being aware of and controlling your emotions by relaxing your body and breathing deeply

Step 2 is to be aware of what triggered the reaction in you or the other person.

- What did you say or do?
- What did they say or do?
- Find out what they think by:

    - Active listening
    - Using open questions, beginning with *What* and *How*, to understand their point of view

- Tell them how you feel and what your concerns are.

Step 3 is to seek closure.

- Create an opportunity for them (or you) to be resourceful or reliable or competent or make a difference (i.e. tapping into their core motivators)
- Look for common ground and a common goal
- Switch to the future – what are we going to do?
- Close the conflict explicitly

If you want to avoid emotional clashes and conflicts with your colleagues, don't appear to challenge their values and

instead act in a way that enables them to get their core needs met, so they maintain their sense of self-worth.

Difficult Conversations

Sometimes conflict can occur because things that started as small tensions or annoyances start to develop into bigger misunderstandings and ultimately conflict. The atmosphere and culture in a team is created by the manager and by the way the members of the team behave. Picking up on unhelpful behaviours is important to create an environment in which people can perform well and be happy.

Most people can sense what is going on in a team, but we do not always trust our senses or act on them. When you notice something that is not quite right, remember that saying nothing is not saying nothing. If you don't say or do anything, then this way of behaving will become accepted practice in the team.

It's especially important to pick up on any behaviour that could be construed as bullying or harassment. Some teams have a culture of "banter." Although the intention might be to have a bit of fun and make work enjoyable, the impact of it on individuals can be negative and can even tip people into feeling victimised or bullied. You have a moral and legal duty to pick up on this type of behaviour.

Nobody likes to deal with difficult situations, and we naturally tend to put off addressing them, hoping they will go away. But deal with them you must, and there are ways to make it easier. Here is a way to plan a conversation with someone whose behaviour has become unacceptable. It's known as the DEFICIT model.[8] Use it to plan the conversation ahead of time. This approach is usually effective in getting the message across and in changing the unwanted behaviour.

DEFICIT Model for a Difficult Conversation

D – Describe the core issue as you see it
E – Evidence – give specific examples
F – Feelings – indicate how **you** feel
I – Implications – what is at stake? What could be the consequences if this doesn't change?

C – Contribution – what part have you played?

I – Intent – what do you want to do?

T – Turn it over – what is their perspective? What might they say? How would you respond?

Once you have planned what you want to say, arrange a meeting, and make your points verbally on all but the last one. While you cannot predict the person's response, it sets the meeting on a positive footing. Mentioning how the behaviour makes you feel has a powerful impact on the person and makes it easier to resolve the problem.

The DEFICIT model can also be useful for dealing with conflict between team members. Conflict in a team is not necessarily a bad thing. In fact, conflict, if managed constructively, can be positive and lead to innovation.

> Honest disagreement is often a good sign of progress. *Mohandas K Gandhi*
>
> For good ideas and true innovation, you need human interaction, conflict, argument, debate. *Margaret Heffernan*

Opinions will differ about whether a discussion is "debate" or "conflict." It's important to create a culture where anyone feels safe to speak up if they feel debate is slipping into conflict (see the section on psychological safety in Chapter 4).

Conflict between team members can be destructive, so it is important to pick up on it and deal with it before it escalates.

TIPS FOR THE TOP MOTIVATORS – DEFUSING CONFLICT

Motivation Pattern	What to Do or Say	What Not to Do or Say
Improviser	"That's so impressive!" "When can you get that done?" Create an opportunity for them to get a quick win and be impressive	"You're not allowed to do that" "The rules say…" "The boss says we have to…" Don't question their resourcefulness

Stabiliser	"I know I can count on you" "What can I do to help you?" Create an opportunity for them to contribute to the task or team	"I can't trust you to do the right thing" "Relax – I'll do it when I can" Don't question their reliability
Theorist	*"How did you get so good at that?"* *"I know you'll work out a way to do it"* Create an opportunity for them to demonstrate their competence	*"This is how you should do it"* *"I'll check up on you at the end of the day"* Don't question their competence
Catalyst	*"I know you care how people feel"* *"We are all in this together"* Create an opportunity for them to make a difference to people	*"You can't really mean that"* *"You're taking it personally"* Don't question their authenticity

Credit to Rob Toomey.

DEVELOPING YOURSELF

Being aware of your own top motivator is a strong foundation for authentic leadership. The four motivation patterns are dynamic, not static – how you fulfil your inner psychological needs and where you direct your motivation varies, depending on your level of maturity and development.[9]

At some points in your development, you may be more concerned with maintaining your self-esteem (feeling that you matter, are respected, and liked[10]), while at other points you may apply your sense of purpose in a broader context, being more concerned with making a difference in your community and contributing to society.[11] See the end-of-chapter references to explore these areas further.

Jack was a senior leader with a successful career. He was attracted to join a company with the vision of transforming itself from being a net carbon polluter to being a key player in the energy transition of the

> planet through the supply of green hydrogen. The business leaders wanted to completely change both how it operated and the products it offered to its customers. This vision connected with Jack's personal sense of purpose to sustain the ecology of the planet for future generations. He wanted to play his part in making a real difference and took a cut in pay to join this organisation. In managing his team, he made time to raise their awareness about the part the company was playing in the energy transition and how their roles contributed to this. He gave them opportunities to develop their own sense of purpose and explore and negotiate how this might connect with the higher purpose the company was pursuing.

It is likely that Jack (above) is expressing his Catalyst motivation pattern and is now applying his core motivator (to fulfil potential) in a broader context, contributing to society.

Someone who is motivated by the need for competence (the Theorist pattern) may find that when they first become a leader, they may be focused on self and proving their competence to others. As they gain experience, they may be more aware of the need to develop competence in their team. When their confidence and abilities grow, they may start to take a broader perspective and build collaborative relationships with others to apply their competence in the service of others and make a difference to their organisation.

At different times you may find that you focus more on some levels, and less on others, in response to changing circumstances. There is no right or wrong – human development does not always proceed in a linear way!

As you are promoted as a leader, remember that what made you successful at one level is going to be different at the next level – doing more of the same won't work; you will need to develop your approach. Managing a team for the first time requires different skills and perspectives from managing other managers, or managing a whole function, division, or business.

The table below illustrates different types and levels of leadership development. It reflects different assumptions about what a leader should be and should do.

- Where are you now in how you relate to your team and colleagues? Tick the statements that are true for you now. These may be at more than one level
- Where would you like to be? Mark statements that reflect how you would like to develop
- How can you get there?

The key to successful leadership is...	My team respecting my authority Making the decisions for my team Ensuring my team wins	
	Being liked by my team Having a happy team Building loyalty	
	Providing the answers Influencing through my knowledge and expertise Having evidence to back my arguments	
	Ensuring people achieve their objectives Building a team of complementary strengths Being true to my own authenticity	
	Seeing issues from different perspectives Influencing change in how people work Generating creative tension or conflict	
	Being of service to followers Transforming constraints Changing my behaviour to suit the needs of the situation	
	Stepping back to gain an external perspective Transforming myself, others, and the organisation Inspiring people by speaking to both their hearts and minds	

Levels of Leadership Development – Credit to Susan Nash, the Type Academy, 12 and Dr Angelina Bennet

You can use many of the tools in this book for your own development. As you become more senior as a leader, you will find that personalised approaches to development are more effective than standard training courses – for example, stretch projects, reflective coaching, and action learning.

Becoming a leader is a lifelong journey – which is what makes it so rewarding!

SUMMARY

As a leader-manager, you are responsible not only for getting the task done but also for managing the human behaviours and relationships, the thoughts and feelings that exist in your team. What you do and say influences how they feel and think. How you connect with your team, whether in meetings or in one-to-one settings, and how you deal with problems, have a massive impact on your team's motivation, performance, and well-being. Being aware of the different motivation patterns and able to flex your approach accordingly give you a head start in leading your team effectively.

You are in a privileged position with the power to influence other people's motivation and well-being. By leading them well, you will not only empower them but also fulfil your own purpose and potential.

ACTION PLAN

Take a few moments to flick back through this book to review your notes and summarise your conclusions: how will you develop yourself as a leader?

What is going well for me as a leader?	
What do I want to do more of?	
How can I make that happen?	
What do I want to do less of?	
How can I make that happen?	
What else?	
What next?	
Who can help?	

A downloadable workbook to accompany the activities in this book is available from www.essenwood.co.uk.

NOTES

1 Syed, M. (2019). *Rebel Ideas: The Power of Diverse Thinking*. London: John Murray.
2 Ibid.
3 Bayne, R. (2004). *Psychological Types at Work: an MBTI Perspective*. London: Thomson.
4 Perlow, L., Hadley, C., and Eun, E. (2017). "Stop the Meeting Madness How to Free Up Time for Meaningful Work." *Harvard Business Review* Vol. 95, No. 4, 62–69.
5 Peters, T. and Waterman, R. (1982). *In Search of Excellence: Lessons from America's Best-Run Companies*. New York: Harper & Row.
6 Hodgson, D. (2012). *Personality in the Classroom*. Carmarthen: Crown House Publishing.
7 Porter, E. (1996). *Relationship Awareness Theory*. 9th edition. Also see Strength Deployment Inventory.
8 Source unknown.
9 Rooke, D. and Torbert, W. (2005). "Seven Transformations of Leadership". *Harvard Business Review* Vol. 83, No. 4, 66–76, 133.
10 Schutz, W. (1958). *FIRO: A Three-Dimensional Theory of Interpersonal Behaviour*. New York: Rinehart.
11 Richard Barrett, Seven Levels of Consciousness Model, https://www.barrettacademy.com/.
12 Susan Nash, The Type Academy, https://type-academy.co.uk/.

APPENDIX

All the practical activities and templates in this book are available in a Workbook, as a free download from the author's website at www.essenwood.co.uk.

APPENDIX CONTENTS

1. A lookup table with the key characteristics of each motivation pattern
2. A summary of the best-known theories of motivation
3. An overview of temperament theory
4. A list of organisations that provide questionnaires to assess temperament and personality type

LOOKUP TABLE OF THE FOUR MOTIVATION PATTERNS

Credit to Linda Berens, Susan Nash, Eve Delunas, Mary McGuinness, David Hodgson.

	Improviser	Stabiliser	Theorist	Catalyst
Their top motivator	**Freedom** To have some choice and control in how they do their job	**Belonging** To belong to the group and feel valued for contributing to it	**Competence** To use their talents and feel they are good at their job	**Potential** To be true to themselves and help others be the best they can be
They value……	Freedom, action, fun, adaptability	Duty, responsibility, consistency, stability	Competence, independence, achievement, learning	Uniqueness, authenticity, harmony, growth
Their core needs are to….	Be noticed. Make an immediate concrete impact Have freedom to act Get impressive quick results	Be responsible Contribute to the group. Have structure and consistency Respect tradition and continuity	Be competent Bring knowledge and expertise Have intellectual independence Contribute to progress	Be authentic Make a difference to others Have purpose or meaning Fulfil potential
What energises them in a job	Troubleshooting, resolving immediate problems	Being part of a team that gets results	Solving complex problems with innovative solutions	Creating solutions that will help people grow

(Continued)

	Improviser	Stabiliser	Theorist	Catalyst
Strengths	Dealing with whatever happens	Making processes work	Designing new processes	Collaborating with others
Challenges	Following routines	Being flexible	Valuing emotions	Being realistic
Skills	Tactical, Adaptable	Logistical, Organised	Strategic, Innovative	Diplomatic, Empathetic
Communication	Brief, casual, humorous	Factual, sequential	Abstract ideas, precise words	Abstract ideas, warm approach
Learns by...	Hands on practice	Repetitive practice	Independent study	Engagement with others
Attitude to change	"What can I do now?"	"If it isn't broken don't fix it"	"Why are we doing this?"	"How will this help people?"
Attitude to feedback	Likes immediate feedback	Likes a physical token	Likes feedback for something they have done	Likes authentic personal feedback
Dislikes, triggers...	Rules and hierarchy; Routine	Disorganisation; Lack of respect for authority	Incompetence; Being told what to think	Insincerity; Disharmony
Stressed by....	Not seeing immediate results; Being confined by rules; Having to wait; Feeling trapped and bored	Not being able to contribute; Constant change; Instability and ambiguity; Feeling left out	Lack of independence; Detailed work with no reason; Repetitive demands; Feeling incompetent	Lack of positive feedback; Doing work with no meaning; Conflict and criticism; Feeling insignificant

	Improviser	Stabiliser	Theorist	Catalyst
How they react to stress	Escalate or retaliate	Blame and complain	Avoid, become preoccupied	Masquerade, disconnect from others
Motto	*"Let's have fun!"*	*"No surprises!"*	*"There's nothing as practical as a good theory"*	*"Be the best you can be"*
As leaders	Tactical, create a fast-moving, fun environment Expect others to react quickly	Logistical, create a planned and orderly environment Expect others to be responsible	Strategic, create an innovative environment Expect others to show initiative	Diplomatic, create a caring, harmonious environment Expect others to collaborate
How they like to be led	Being free to respond to the needs of the moment Short term deadlines and clear actions	With clear plans and regular check-ins on progress Being part of a team effort	Being allowed independence in how they achieve their tasks Having an opportunity to learn	With a warm, personal approach By someone with integrity and authenticity

MOTIVATION THEORIES

> Nothing is as practical as a good theory. *Kurt Lewin*[1]

This is a brief overview of some of the most important academic theories related to motivation.

Most motivation theories broadly fall into two categories: the *content* of WHAT motivates us, which gives us a sense of purpose and reason for doing something; and the *processes* of HOW we are motivated.

Content Theories

Universal Human Needs

There are some universal needs that all humans share and that we are naturally motivated to fulfil – they give us purpose and drive our actions.

These are the universal needs to:

- Stay alive (survive)
- Have relationships with other people
- Grow and develop (thrive)

These needs can all be present simultaneously.

The diagram from Alderfer (Figure A.1) shows these three levels of need and is sometimes known as the ERG theory.[2]

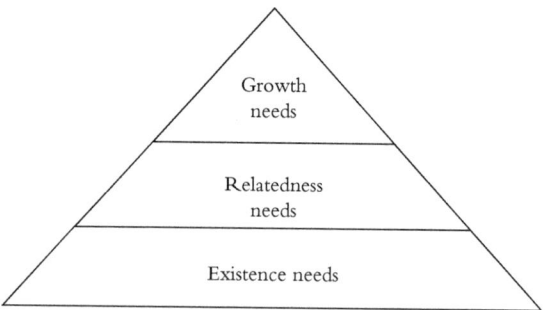

Figure A.1 ERG Theory

Maslow's hierarchy of needs[3] is similar, with physiological and safety needs at the bottom, moving through needs for love and belonging, to self-esteem and finally to growth through self-actualisation at the top of his pyramid.

Motivation at Work

Herzberg's[4] Two-Factor Theory

This divides the things that people want from their jobs into two categories:

- "Motivators" (e.g. interesting work, recognition, responsibility, opportunities for growth, achievement)
- "Hygiene factors" – things that don't actually motivate you but can cause dissatisfaction if they are not sufficient (e.g. salary, benefits, conditions, job security)

The good news for leader-managers is that you usually have influence over the motivators.

Herzberg also made a distinction between extrinsic and intrinsic motivation:

> I can charge a person's battery, and then recharge it, and recharge it again. But it is *only when one has a generator of one's own that we can talk about motivation*. One then needs no outside stimulation. One *wants* to do it.

Self-Determination Theory

Self-Determination Theory[5] describes three fundamental human needs for:

- Autonomy (being able to choose what we do)
- Competence (belief that we know what we are doing)
- Relatedness (having fulfilling and secure relationships)

If these needs are met, we are more likely to feel motivated and have a sense of well-being.

Dan Pink[6] draws on this theory in his book and writes about needs for autonomy, mastery, and purpose.

McClelland's[7] Motivation Theory

This theory suggests that needs are learned from the culture of a society. Once learned, these needs – for either achievement, power, or affiliation – influence how individuals pursue their goals.

Self-Concept Theory[8]

This suggests that people are motivated when what they do fits with their self-concept, and they get an opportunity for self-esteem and self-worth.

Process Theories

These theories are concerned with the *processes* of HOW we are motivated.

Goal Setting[9]

This well-known theory has been adopted in many organisations and is covered in Chapter 5.

Social Cognitive Theory[10]

This theory proposes that people's confidence that they have the ability to do something (known as "self-efficacy") determines their level of motivation. The impact of thoughts and beliefs on motivation is covered in Chapter 5.

Other Process Theories

Expectancy theory[11]
Equity theory[12]
Flow[13]

Differential emotions theory[14]
Positive emotions[15]
Attribution theory[16]

OVERVIEW OF TEMPERAMENT THEORY

The idea of **four core motivators** has a long history dating back to 450 BC when Hippocrates described the four "temperaments" – patterns of human behaviour – and named them choleric, phlegmatic, melancholic, and sanguine. These ideas were well known for hundreds of years – in the Middle Ages, Chaucer used these words to describe some of the pilgrims in *The Canterbury Tales*. Hippocrates, and Chaucer, believed that behaviour and personality were caused by different fluids circulating around the body.

Things have moved on a bit since then, and we no longer believe there are fluids in the body that drive our behaviour. But neuroscientists have demonstrated that there are chemical and hormonal links between body and mind which influence behaviour.[17]

Traits or Patterns?

Temperament describes *patterns* of behaviour rather than breaking behaviour down into individual traits. In the 20th century, most psychologists took a "trait" approach to personality, but two German psychologists (Ernst Kretschmer[18] and Eduard Spränger[19]) looked at *patterns* of behaviour. David Keirsey[20] drew on their work and updated the ancient ideas about temperament. Subsequently, Linda Berens[21] renamed the temperaments as "essential motivators." These ideas have stood the test of time and endured because they make sense to people and help them understand themselves and others.

Both approaches to personality – looking at either individual traits or overall patterns – can be useful, depending on what you want to do. In day-to-day life, I find looking at *patterns* of behaviour is helpful, both in understanding myself and in working and living with other people. If I think of one of my friends, I picture her as a whole person, I don't think of her as a set of individual characteristics. It is the configuration of a variety of factors that represent someone's personality.[22]

Think about a lion and a leopard (Figure A.2 (a) and (b)).

(a)   (b)

Figure A.2 Trait or Type?

Lions and leopards share certain traits – they are in the cat family, they are furry, they stalk and kill their prey, they are carnivorous, they run quickly, and so on. But when you look at them holistically, they are quite different from each other. The images of a whole lion or a whole leopard are more helpful to me in knowing what to expect than knowing their individual traits. Similarly, if I buy a new car, I tell my friends I have bought "a Nissan Qashqai." This gives them an immediate picture of the car – if I said I had bought something with alloy tyres, a V6 engine, and a sunroof, they would not have such a clear idea of the car I had bought.

It is the same with the temperament patterns in people. It is their whole self which has an impact on me, rather than their individual traits.

Description or Prediction?

No model of personality explains everything about human behaviour but grouping people who share certain characteristics together helps us make sense of ourselves and of them while recognising that we also have many individual differences, and we develop over time. How we behave in the world (by behaviour, I mean what we do, say, think, and feel) is influenced by many things in addition to our inborn personality. Our upbringing, education, experiences, the culture in which we live, our circumstances, the work we do, all influence our behaviour, and we almost always have a choice in how we behave. In addition, psychologists are now recognising that **personality is both stable and malleable**.

Temperament *describes* how someone might behave but does not *predict* their behaviour in all circumstances. We can display different behaviours (and traits) in different situations, and we can change them too.[23] On the nurture versus nature debate, studies of twins suggest that about 50% of our traits can be traced to differences in genes and 50% can be traced to different environments. Personality is not fixed – it is malleable, and traits can and do change, especially through big life events such as a first relationship. Paradoxically, it seems that "traits are stable and also dynamic and changeable."[24]

Temperament helps explain why we do what we do – it is a set of underlying core needs and values that influence how we behave – but it does not limit us. The underlying needs may remain, but how we express them in our behaviour and where we direct our sense of purpose can change, as we grow and develop to become more rounded human beings.

Temperament also helps us understand other people. While we see other people's behaviour, we do not always know what core needs might be driving it. Similarly, we are not always aware of our own core needs and values that underpin our motivation pattern. If we are more aware of them, we can make life choices that are more likely to enable us to grow, develop, fulfil our potential, and have a sense of well-being and contentment as we move through life.

SELF-ASSESSMENT QUESTIONNAIRES

The following organisations provide questionnaires to assess temperament. You may have to contract with a qualified practitioner to access them.

TypeCoach: https://www.type-coach.com/

Keirsey: https://www.keirsey.com/

Step Research: https://stepresearch.com/ or https://www.PersonalityWizard.com for a free report

Career/Life Skills Resources: https://www.clsr.ca/product-category/personality-dimensions/

NOTES

1 *Human Resource Development Review* Vol. 4, No. 2, 111–113, June 2005.
2 Alderfer, C. (1972). *Existence, Relatedness, and Growth: Human Needs in Organizational Settings.* New York: Free Press.

3. Maslow, A. (1943). "A Theory of Human Motivation." *Psychological Review* Vol. 50, 370–396.
4. Herzberg, F. (1968). "One More Time: How Do You Motivate Employees?" *Harvard Business Review Harvard Business Review*, Vol. 46, 53–62.
5. Ryan, R. and Deci, L. (2000) "Self-Determination Theory and the Facilitation of Intrinsic Motivation, Social Development, and Well-being." *American Psychologist* Vol. 55, No. 1, 68–78.
6. Pink, D. (2009). *Drive: The Surprising Truth about What Motivates Us*. New York: Riverhead Books.
7. McClelland, D. (1961). *The Achieving Society*. Princeton, NJ: D. Van Nostrand Co.
8. Shamir, B., House, R. and Arthur, M. (1993). "The Motivational Effects of Charismatic Leadership: A Self-concept Based Theory." *Organization Science* Vol. 4, 577–594.
9. Locke, E. and Latham, G. (1990). *A Theory of Goal Setting & Task Performance*. Englewood Cliffs, NJ: Prentice Hall.
10. Bandura, A. (1977). "Self-efficacy: Toward a Unifying Theory of Behavioral Change." *Psychological Review* Vol. 84, No. 2, 191–215.
11. Vroom, V. (1964). *Work and Motivation*. New York: Wiley and Sons.
12. Adams, J. S. (1963). "Productivity and Work Quality as a Function of Wage Inequities". *Industrial Relations: A Journal of Economy and Society* Vol. 3, No. 1, 9–16.
13. Csikszentmihalyi, M. (1990). *Flow: The Psychology of Optimal Experience*. New York: Harper Collins.
14. Izard, C. E. (1989). "The Structure and Functions of Emotions: Implications for Cognition, Motivation, and Personality." In I. S. Cohen (Ed.), *The G. Stanley Hall Lecture Series* (pp. 39–73). American Psychological Association.
15. Fredrickson, B. (2004). "The Broaden-and-Build Theory of Positive Emotions." *Philosophical Transactions of the Royal Society of London*.
16. Weiner, B. (1986). *An Attributional Theory of Motivation and Emotion*. New York: Springer-Verlag.
17. Boschi, H. (2020). *Why We Do What We Do: Understanding our Brain to Get the Best Out of Ourselves and Others*. Chichester: Wiley.
18. Kretschmer, E. (1925). *Physique and Character*. New York: Harcourt Brace.
19. Spranger, E. (1928). *Types of Men*. Halle (Saale): Niemeyer.
20. Keirsey, D. and Bates, M. (1978). *Please Understand Me: Character and Temperament Types*. Del Mar, CA: Prometheus Nemesis.
21. Berens, L. (2019). *Understanding Yourself and Others™ Exploring Essential Motivators™*. www.interstrength.org.
22. Levitin, D. (2020). *Successful Ageing: A Neuroscientist Explores the Power and Potential of Our Lives*. New York: Dutton.
23. Ibid.
24. Prof. Weibke Bleidorn interviewed by Katya Adler for One to One on BBC Radio 4, 12 May 2020.

INDEX

Adair, John 26, 81
Alderfer, C. 15

Bandura, A. 22
banter 96, 165
BEAR Chain, 108
Beckham, David 55
beliefs 107–109
belonging 6, 19–21, 43, 45–46, 54–56, 98, 102, 141, 147, 150, 155, 173; Connect to create 92–97, 99, 146; *see also* Stabiliser motivation pattern
Berens, Linda 20, 44, 179
Bishop, Catherine 17
boredom 17, 29, 132
brainstorming 62, 66, 72, 122
bullying 165
burnout 131

Campbell, Joseph 31
Catalyst motivation pattern 20, 42, 44–46, 64, 67, 74, 77, 98–99, 122, 142, 147, 150, 155–156, 161–163, 167–168, 173–175; challenges 69–71, 174; communication style 73, 174; inner drive 68; job requirements 71–73, 173; talents and strengths 68–69, 174; *see also* potential
coaching 103, 116–122, 124

communication styles 53–54, 60–61, 66–67, 73, 93–94, 120, 150–152, 159–161, 174
competence 6, 19–21, 43, 45–46, 61, 64, 66, 98, 102, 142, 147, 150, 155, 173; Develop to build 85–89, 99, 146; *see also* Theorist motivation pattern
confidence 23, 103, 105–108
conflict management 145, 161–167
Connect, to create belonging 75, 76, 92–97, 99, 146
core motivators 6, 19–22, 31–32, 43–44, 47, 74–77, 79, 84, 97–99, 121–124, 140–143, 145–150, 159–161, 166–167, 173–175, 179; *see also individual motivators*
Covey, Stephen 139
COVID-19 3, 18, 48, 84, 133, 157

Danckert, J. 17
Darwin, Charles 9
Deci, L. 19–20
DEFICIT model 165–166
Delegate, to give freedom 75, 76, 90–92, 99, 146
demands 10–11
demotivation 14, 89, 102, 111, 133
Develop, to build competence 75, 76, 85–89, 99, 146
difficult conversations 145, 165–166
disruptive behaviours 156–157

Djokovic, Novak 106
drives 10–11

Eastwood, J. 17
Einstein, Albert 62
emotions 107–109, 127, 130–132, 162–164
empathy 34, 68–69, 96, 135–136
energy 127–132
energy bias 152–155
Engage, to give meaning 75, 76–85, 146
ERG theory 176–177
extraverts 53, 59, 66, 72, 151, 153–155, 158–159
extrinsic motivation 11, 77, 177

feedback 22, 28, 85, 89, 103, 113–116, 120–122, 124, 160–161, 174
freedom 6, 19–21, 43, 45–46, 48, 50–51, 53, 98, 102, 141, 147, 150, 155, 173; Delegate to give 90–92, 99, 146; *see also* Improviser motivation pattern

Gandhi, Mohandas 68, 166
Gen Z 4
goal setting 22–23, 103, 109–113, 120–122, 124, 129, 178
Goldilocks principle 110
Grant, Adam 47
GROW model 117–120

habits: healthy 129; helpful 135, 137–138
Heffernan, Margaret 166
Herzberg, F. 177
hierarchy of needs 19, 177
Holmes, Kelly 104
home working 3, 133, 136, 140
hybrid working 3–4, 136, 140

Improviser motivation pattern 20, 42–43, 45–46, 57, 90, 98–99, 122, 140–141, 147, 149–150, 155–156, 159, 162–163, 166, 173–175; challenges 50–51, 174; communication style 53–54, 174; inner drive 48; job requirements 51–53, 173; talents and strengths 48–50, 174; *see also* freedom
individual purpose 82–85
information bias 152, 155–156
intrinsic motivation 10–11, 77, 177
introverts 53, 59–60, 66, 72, 151, 153–155, 158
Izard, Carroll 77

Jobs, Steve 62
Jung, Carl 62, 153

Keirsey, David 179
Kolb, David 86
Kotter, John 24
Kretschmer, Ernst 179

Latham, G. 22
leader-managers' role 24–28, 109–121, 134–140; coaching 103, 116–122, 124; feedback 22, 28, 85, 89, 103, 113–116, 120–122, 124, 160–161, 174; goal setting 22–23, 103, 109–113, 120–122, 124, 129, 178; listening 135–136, 164; prioritising 135, 139–140; role modelling 135–136
leadership styles 145–151, 170; conflict management 161–166; developing yourself 167–170; engaging with your team 151–159; tips for top motivators 159–161, 166–167; *see also* leader-managers' role; management
Learning Cycle 85–86, 115
Levitin, David 16
listening 135–136, 164
Locke, E. 22

Maestas, Nicole 16
management: and creating purpose (*see* purpose); and motivation 3–6;

and well-being 4–5; *see also* leader-managers' role; leadership styles
managing by wandering around 136, 158
Mandela, Nelson 68
Maslow, Abraham 19, 177
Mayo, Andrew 77
McClelland, D. 178
meetings 145, 152–156; virtual 152, 156–159
mental health 4, 29, 129; *see also* stress; well-being
mentoring 121, 123
Merton, Paul 49
mindfulness 129–130
Mirren, Helen 49
motivation: core motivators (*see* core motivators; *individual motivators*); definition of 10–13; extrinsic 11, 77, 177; intrinsic 10–11, 77, 177; leadership styles 145–170 (*see also* leader-managers' role); management and 3–6; motivation equation 111–112; purpose (*see* purpose); self-motivation 3, 29, 31 (*see also* purpose); sustaining (*see* persistence, resilience); theories 19–20, 176–181; top motivators (*see* core motivators); and well-being 14–15, 19; why you need motivation 1–2

performance mapping 87–89
persistence 12, 22–23, 28, 76, 102, 117, 126; creating a culture of 121; definition of 13, 103–109; leader-managers' role 109–121; tips for top motivators 121–124
Pink, Dan 178
potential, fulfilling 6, 19–21, 44–46, 67–68, 98, 102–105, 142, 147, 150, 155, 173; *see also* Catalyst motivation pattern
prioritising 135, 139–140
process theories 178–179

psychological safety 95–96
Pugh, Lewis 18, 22
purpose 12, 14, 23, 28–29, 31–32, 76, 102, 126; definition of 10, 13; individual purpose 82–85; quiz 37–45; self-insight activities 32–36; team purpose 77–82; tips for top motivators 97–99; why you need purpose 15–19

resilience 12, 22–24, 28–29, 76, 102, 126, 143; definition of 13, 127; energy 127–132; leader-managers' role 134–140; and stress 132–134; tips for top motivators 140–143
rewards 10–11
role modelling 135–136
Ruskin, John 1
Ryan, R. 19–20

self-actualisation 19–20; *see also* potential
self-assessment questionnaires 181
self-belief 104–105; coaching to build 116–121
self-concept theory 178
self-determination theory 19–20, 177–178
self-efficacy 22–23
self-insight activities 32–36
self-motivation 3, 29, 31; *see also* purpose
Sinek, Simon 15
SMART/SMARTER goals 22, 110–112
social cognitive theory 178
Spränger, Eduard 179
Stabiliser motivation pattern 20, 42–43, 45–46, 51, 93, 98–99, 122, 141, 147, 150, 155–156, 160, 162–163, 167, 173–175; challenges 57–58, 174; communication style 60–61, 174; inner drive 54–55; job requirements 58–60, 173; talents

and strengths 55–56, 174; *see also* belonging
Stop-Start-Continue template 115, 151
stress 29, 96, 131–134, 174–175
Syed, Matthew 146

team purpose 77–82
temperament theory 179–181
Theorist motivation pattern 20, 42–43, 45–46, 57–58, 71, 85, 98–99, 122, 130, 142, 147, 149–150, 155–156, 160, 162–163, 167–168, 173–175; challenges 63–64, 174; communication style 66–67, 174; inner drive 61–62; job requirements 64–66, 173; talents and strengths 62–63, 174; *see also* competence

Three Ps Model of Effective Teamwork 152–156
top motivators *see* core motivators
trust, building 93, 97
Tsitsipas, Stefanos 107
two-factor theory 177

Urgent-Important Matrix 139–140

virtual coaching 120–121
virtual meetings 152, 156–159

well-being 1, 4–5, 14–15, 19, 29, 76, 127; *see also* mental health
Whitlock, Max 22
Whitmore, John 117
Wicks, Joe 49
work–life balance 1, 23, 133

Ingram Content Group UK Ltd.
Milton Keynes UK
UKHW050224240623
423724UK00054B/484